O
3/12
4/12

4
1/15

3/07/12

THE THINGS YOU WOULD HAVE SAID

THE THINGS
YOU WOULD
HAVE SAID

The Chance
to Say What You
Always Wanted
Them to Know

Jackie Hooper

HUDSON
STREET
PRESS

HUDSON STREET PRESS
Published by the Penguin Group

Penguin Group (USA) Inc., 375 Hudson Street, New York, New York 10014, U.S.A. •
Penguin Group (Canada), 90 Eglinton Avenue East, Suite 700, Toronto, Ontario, Canada
M4P 2Y3 (a division of Pearson Penguin Canada Inc.) • Penguin Books Ltd., 80 Strand,
London WC2R 0RL, England • Penguin Ireland, 25 St. Stephen's Green, Dublin 2,
Ireland (a division of Penguin Books Ltd.) • Penguin Group (Australia), 250 Camber-
well Road, Camberwell, Victoria 3124, Australia (a division of Pearson Australia Group
Pty. Ltd.) • Penguin Books India Pvt. Ltd., 11 Community Centre, Panchsheel Park,
New Delhi – 110 017, India • Penguin Group (NZ), 67 Apollo Drive, Rosedale, Auckland
0632, New Zealand (a division of Pearson New Zealand Ltd.) • Penguin Books (South
Africa) (Pty.) Ltd., 24 Sturdee Avenue, Rosebank, Johannesburg 2196, South Africa

Penguin Books Ltd., Registered Offices: 80 Strand, London WC2R 0RL, England

First published by Hudson Street Press, a member of Penguin Group (USA) Inc.

First Printing, March 2012
1   3   5   7   9   10   8   6   4   2

Some of the selections first appeared on The Things You Would Have Said website.

REGISTERED TRADEMARK—MARCA REGISTRADA

LIBRARY OF CONGRESS CATALOGING-IN-PUBLICATION DATA

The things you would have said : the chance to say what you always wanted
them to know / Jackie Hooper [compiler].
p. cm.
ISBN 978-1-59463-086-6 (hardcover : alk. paper)
1. American letters.   I. Hooper, Jackie.
PN6131.T45 2012
816.008—dc23   2011029821

Printed in the United States of America
Set in Tactile ITC Std and Felbridge Std Light • Designed by Chris Welch

To my parents

Thank you for giving me a voice,
so I can help others find their own.

Contents

Introduction

I have spent the last few years collecting letters from complete strangers.

It began in March 2009, after the actress Natasha Richardson died suddenly of complications from a minor skiing accident. I was on vacation with my family in Hawaii when I heard the news of her passing. I glanced at the television while searching for my flip-flops and froze in my steps. Natasha had been on vacation, trying to conquer a new activity, when a freak accident ended her life. At that moment, our lives were eerily similar and I was struck by the disturbing realization that I was also on vacation, also trying new things. What if something happened to my dad during a scuba trip or to my niece during her first swim in the ocean? As my family and I gathered our sunglasses and magazines, I felt a strange sense of shame come over me, almost as though I should feel guilty for being able to enjoy a vacation with my family while something terrible was happening to hers.

Even after arranging our deck chairs and settling around the pool, I couldn't stop thinking about Natasha. I kept thinking about her family and friends who assumed they would hear her voice later that night or see her for the dinner party they had planned. I thought about how quickly our lives can change and how the people we expect to be around indefinitely can disappear in an instant.

Sometimes, in the wake of a natural disaster, ordinary people feel compelled to fly across the world to provide relief. I was beginning to feel something similar. It wasn't enough to appreciate what I had in my own life and go about my day; I wanted to help people find a way to cope with life-altering moments. I wanted to somehow give them a chance to speak to a loved one once more, to have that final conversation. I knew I couldn't provide a face-to-face interaction, but I thought I could offer them the next best thing.

I sat silently for a moment before turning to my parents and saying, "What if I started collecting letters from people, asking them to write to someone and say something they've always wanted to say? It could be an outlet for people." While they nodded appropriately and were equally encouraging, I don't think they fully understood what I was envisioning, nor the urgency I felt in beginning this project. I didn't even know what I would do with the letters yet, but I did know that writers would feel encouraged if they felt that others cared about what they had to say. After a few minutes, I went back inside and opened my laptop.

By the time I returned to the mainland, I had a list of organizations to contact that would enable me to reach a fair amount of people at one time. The question I wanted to ask was simple: If you were given the chance to tell someone something you never had the opportunity to express, what would it be? I wrote to schools, jails, retirement homes, and churches around my community, attempting to include people of all ages and backgrounds. I wanted the project to prove that no matter your age or life experience, there is always something you wish you could have said, no matter how big or small it might be. I tried not to form any expectations for what this was to become or how many people I would reach; I just knew I simply had to try. After the first positive responses to my inquiries started to arrive, it confirmed that others, too, thought it was worth a try, and that was all I had been hoping for.

One of my first presentations was to a church congregation two hours south of my hometown. After I posted my homemade flyers on the bulletin board in the lobby, I sat alone in a pew and waited for the pastor to call me to the front of the crowd. I was nervous, wondering if anyone would listen or participate, since I was not a member of the congregation. However, when I finished speaking and sat back down, members began whispering to me, leaning over one another and asking for my e-mail and how they could learn more about the project. Following the service, people spoke of loved ones in the hospital and told me stories about their lives. When I left that morning, I was thrilled. I felt as though I had connected with people and was starting to make my mark. But a few days passed, and the letters I was expecting didn't arrive. I felt discouraged and began to question whether I'd had any impact at all.

Soon, though, I received a letter that would serve as one of the most significant reminders of my motivation for the project. It was from a man at the church. He'd written to a high school classmate who was killed in a hit-and-run accident. Back then, the boy had often been harassed for being gay, which the writer noticed but did little to stop, and in the letter, the writer admitted his fear that the boy's death was the result of such bullying. He wrote, "Here it is, forty-three years later, and I still think about what I did not do." For the first time, I truly understood the importance of the project. It was not just my little idea anymore—other people were relying on me now, and it was up to me to make their stories heard. This is it, I thought. This is what it is all about.

As I began gathering even more submissions from the presentations, I was continually taken aback by the letters I received. The rawness of the pain being expressed was heartbreaking, and the honesty was humbling. Wives angrily wondered why their husbands had taken their own lives, mothers apologized to their never-born children. However, writers were also expressing much more than sorrow and pain. Students thanked former teachers for the valuable lessons learned in class, kids asked old neighbors questions about their new life and friends, and both men and women relived awkward moments they experienced in high school. I found myself smiling, even laughing at times, when I had initially expected to only be fighting back tears. The writers gave this project a new life, a bigger life, in unexpected and inspiring ways.

While I continued to reach out to local organizations, I quickly realized that a great deal of people could benefit from the project beyond my immediate community. Thus, I created a blog, www.wouldhavesaid.com, and began to post one letter each day. I hoped that through the Web site others could learn about the project, read submissions, and become inspired to write a letter of their own. Again the response was overwhelming. I received e-mails from Chicago, Florida, Quebec, and Finland, with letters of vivid memories and untold stories overflowing my inbox. Though I had hoped people could relate to this idea and participate in the project, I never could have predicted the impact it has had.

Often sent along with the letters are personal notes to me that say, "Thank you for giving people like me a chance to have a voice." Writers say that by sending their letter to me, they truly feel as if they are sending the letter to the person they've written to; they often add, "And now that I've let it out, I can let it go." The release is so powerful, in fact, that many people send in a second or third or even fourth letter. Readers, too, are deeply touched by the project, saying how each new letter gives them "a fresh perspective on life in an almost indescribable way."

Even now, I am still amazed by the letters I receive. I find myself in awe of just how many people are willing to write about feelings they may not have even shared with those closest to them; how simply knowing you have an audience who cares and is willing to listen can inspire powerful expression. It has been a profound demonstration of people's ability and desire to connect with one another during the difficult moments in life, reaching out to each other like old friends. It might take a moment for the idea to sink in, and it might take the writers some time to sort through their thoughts, but their follow-through has reminded me of the courage that lies in so many of us, even when we might not yet realize it is there.

I hope you fall in love with these letters, just as I have, and will be touched by their words. I hope their strength inspires you.

FRIENDS,
OR
SOMETHING
LIKE IT

~

Dear Susan,

　　We are organizing our thirty-year class reunion for this coming summer, and you're on the "lost list." It doesn't surprise me; after the way we all treated you, I cannot imagine that you would ever want to see us again, much less to share the intimate details of your life since leaving high school.

　　We were terrible to you. More particularly, I was terrible to you.

　　Back in junior high, when you first moved here, we became fast friends. After having gone to school with the same cohort of kids my entire life, it was refreshing to meet someone new. It didn't matter to me that you lived in a mobile home or that your parents were older and didn't have much money. It didn't matter to me that you wore geeky clothes. It mattered that we were friends.

　　That is, it mattered until a more popular group of girls began making fun of you. I badly wanted their acceptance, so I went along with it. One day, I stopped talking to you entirely. I can still remember sitting there stony-faced at lunchtime while you cried and begged me to tell you what you had done wrong. The truth is, you had done nothing wrong. Your only "crime" was being undesirable to those I wanted to accept me.

After that, you had no friends at all for a time. When you found your niche in the Civil Air Patrol group, this unfortunately only gained you additional ridicule as we all began calling you "Susie Air Force" and laughing at your shiny patent leather pumps when you wore your uniform to school. The last I knew, you intended to enter the Air Force following graduation.

I've thought of you many times over the years and feel so bad for having been what can only be described as a cold bitch. I am so sorry. I hope that someday I will have the opportunity to tell you this in person and that you can forgive me. At a time when we all had tremendous angst in our young lives and were trying to figure out who we were as individuals, I made your life worse. You didn't need that, and I not only dishonored our friendship, I dishonored the concept of friendship in general. From this I learned that one's true friends do not tie such strings to a relationship. For all it cost me, and by extension you, I have not kept in touch with any of those girls since high school and they no longer figure in my life. You, however, do. I have never forgotten this lesson learned and I strive to treat people better as a result. I truly hope you have gone on to enjoy a good life and that our horrible behavior back in school has not enduringly colored your existence. Be well, my friend.

Love,
Debbie, age 47

Boy,

I miss you. I miss the little things and the big things and the in-between things. I miss your stupid smile and the laugh you used to give me when you finally got me back with sarcasm. I miss your stupid lisp that popped up out of nowhere just to piss me off. I miss leaving the library to go study at your house instead. I miss the stupid goddamn car that I hated, and I miss the way it smelled. I miss you bringing me takeout and calling me to ask if you put ice in sweet tea. I miss how you had a sheet nailed to your wall, your mattress on the floor, and the lone can of Ragú in your closet.

I miss sneaking out of my dorm to do absolutely nothing with you. I miss driving back to take my final and failing it because I sat in your arms all night. I miss the first, the second, and all the other good-byes we had. I miss talking while the rain poured down, and I miss sleeping in your arms because I fit there just right. I miss your ugly comforter and the fact that you had no sheets. I miss your cologne and how gross you smelled when it got hotter than sixty degrees outside.

I miss your drunken calls to me at three a.m. and the heartbreak that always ensued. I miss your cat that hated me and the way you touched my hair. I miss sitting in a gas station parking lot at four a.m. and talking about hurt. I miss you telling me that I can do anything I want. I miss you calling me when I screamed at you for hours, just to ask me if I was done being angry.

I miss hating you, because it was easier than missing you.

Girl, age 18

Dear Violet,

I wish I would have told you how much you make me feel overjoyed. Every time we saw each other, we would run to one another and embrace in a great big hug. I am so sorry that sometimes I forced you to do things that you didn't want to do.

I wish I could have said good-bye when I had the chance. Now that we are older, the chance that we will see each other again is growing thinner and thinner each passing day. I regret never asking to play again. How did we ever lose touch?

I still have you in my heart and on the refrigerator. The picture of us is the only memory of you I have left. I hope you still have the picture, too. I wonder, and hope, you still remember me.

Your friend,

Sarah, age 10

Dear Clive,

It has been almost twenty years since you decided you could not handle the world anymore. You left my sister, your son and my family forever. I remember how strong a man you seemed to be when I first met you: the motivation you had, and how, when I came over to England at only thirteen years old, you protected me from that strange guy who was sticking his nose where it didn't belong.

I know your business failures weighed heavily on you, and how you must have felt despair when the bills were coming in and you guys were barely making it. I wish I could have been old enough to step in and do something. Now, I just feel emptiness in losing someone I could relate to.

You should see your son. He was accepted into a very elite maintenance program at the age of sixteen, beating out people many times his senior. He is living on his own. Such a success. He still remembers and misses you so much.

I wish I could have gone around England one more time. Instead, every time I hear the Genesis song "Fading Lights," I think about what might have been had you just held on and reached out for help.

From,
Your brother-in-law, age 34

⌒

To Gilly,

You were the best dog I've ever had and the most reliable constant in my life. I'm so sorry I wasn't there for you when you fell asleep and never woke up. I should have been that person there with you; I should have given you my warmth like how you gave me your warmth when you jumped up to my bed every night. You made me feel comfortable and safe.

Your beauty came from both the inside and out, and I will never see another dog and not think of you. You brought our household together and showed us that it was okay to show some sort of affection to one another. Gilly, you gave me a reason to go home. You got excited every time I walked in the door, running up and wagging your tail as if you hadn't seen me for years. Now I find it hard even thinking about my childhood home without you. You were my full-time friend and although you couldn't express your feelings through words, I could see it in your beautiful orange-green eyes. The other day I found a jacket that still had "Gilly hair" on it; your white hair was so easy to spot. You deserved me being there at the end. You deserved it, but I wasn't.

I could see you getting old, limping and having less and less energy every day. I should have known to stay when you wouldn't even eat your favorite treats anymore. I will always remember you, my friend. I would be lucky to find a dog or friend as reliable and amazing as you.

Thank you for being a part of my life,

Meg, age 21

⌢

Anthony,

When you hurt me or push me, I wish I could tell you to not do that. You whacked me with a hose and I wish I could tell you how I felt. That is why I have a scar. You hated me and I wanted to be friends with you. Next time I see you, I hope you apologize to me. I hope you will be a better man when I see you next time.

Josh, age 10

⌢

Dear Daniel,

Not everyone has to experience riding the bus to school, and they don't know how hard bus life can be when you're in high school. I was just a scared freshman, waiting on the wrong side of the road for a bus I had never seen before, and then you walked up. You made me laugh and told me who not to sit by. Every morning the whole bus was woken up by the sounds of our laughter as we got on the bus. I had some of my best times riding the bus to and from school because of you.

But then you had to move. Then I was alone on the bus trying to continue the legacy you made. We still talked on the phone and e-mailed each other, but it wasn't the same. I missed your big smile and the joy you brought to my life. I didn't realize how much I missed it until you were gone.

Almost a year to the day of your move I got that phone call telling me you had jumped to your death. I didn't believe it. Not my Daniel. To this day, almost four years later, I still think about you and smile at all the good times we had. But I know those days are over.

You were my best friend, Daniel, and I may never come to terms with the reasons you would want to leave this earth at eighteen, but I want you to know that I can never forget you. I want my questions answered so badly that I pray for a dream that will let me talk to you. A dream that would just give me some peace, to know that you are happy where you are.

Shenade, age 21

⌒

Dear Sister,

I am so sorry I was not able to be with you every step of the way while you were going through treatment.

I am so sorry I was not able to be with you each time you found out the cancer had returned. I know you called me every time and I was able to talk to you on the phone, but it's not the same as being with you, holding your hand when you received the devastating news, which you had to hear on four different occasions.

I am so proud of how courageous you were for yourself, your sons and your friends during your five-year battle with cancer. You always managed to keep your spirits up and even find humor in what must have been some terrifying times for you.

After we lost you, everyone I talked with had so many wonderful things to say about you and your spirit. Your doctor told me that even though he deals with death every day, your death had been especially hard for him. He told me how when you were in chemotherapy, you would laugh and talk with all the other patients and make their time there so much easier. He said how greatly you would be missed.

I am so glad I was able to be with you at the end, though. You were still laughing and joking and being yourself. That time was precious to me. You were my friend, my sister and my confidante and I miss you every day.

I hope you and Jimmy are in heaven watching how strong and responsible your two boys are. They have been dealt such a hard time in their short lives, first to lose their father when they were so young and now, just fifteen years later, to lose their mother. They were always so proud of you. They adored you.

I will say good-bye now, my friend. I just wished I could have done more for you while you were here.

Your sister, age 52

Dear new fish,

I hope you enjoy your new house. I don't have a pet that can eat you. You are going to be in my room. You can watch me sleep. It will be awesome. I won't ignore you. I won't let anything dangerous happen to you.

Love,

Ethan, age 8

Dear Friend,

I remember when we became friends back in high school. You were a gift from God. I had a few friends at school but you were my only friend outside of school, and you were pretty much the only one who understood me. I could make you laugh and that made me feel good. I asked you out once, but you said no. I think you were probably scared for the same reasons I was: that it would ruin an important friendship we had.

In college, we went to separate schools five hours apart, but we still managed to remain friends and even get together when we were both in town. After getting turned down in high school, I never did ask you out again, partly because I was scared of getting rejected again and partly because I didn't want to mess up the friendship we had worked so hard to protect.

We are both married now, happily so. I would never choose anyone over my wife and I love her more than the world. However, I've always wanted to say that I do love you. Back in high school, it was an infatuation kind of love. In college, it became a more mature type of love that I was scared to act on. Now, it is an appreciative love. I realize what a great friendship we had and I look back on it with fondness.

We don't talk much now because we both have our own lives, but I have always wanted to tell you that I love you.

Nick, age 28

Dear Baby,

I'll come back to you. Don't lose faith. I didn't know I'd be gone so long. You're mine, and I miss you so much. Don't forget the cinnamon rolls or the toothpaste kisses, dancing to Bon Jovi or summer road trips. Don't forget to read every night and don't forget to say your prayers. Most of all, don't forget sister love.

Remember,

Sisi, age 18

⁓

Dear Allison,

I was completely blindsided when you stopped talking to me and started talking about me. I'm not really sure what it was that made you think I'd changed—because I'm not so sure that it was *me* who changed—but I do know that it hurt.

Best friends for twelve years, and you can't even find it in your heart to tell me what made you think so lowly of me?

It hurts.

At first I was angry. I was going through a hard time, you knew it, and you decided that now would be the time to turn your back on me. It had only been a few days prior that you were writing sentimental things in my yearbook, reliving the past few years when we had been completely attached at the hip. That was almost three months ago.

I still don't know why you turned so hostile towards me, but I like to think that I've grown a little more mature because of it. I'm leaving in thirteen days, and I don't know when I'll be back. But I do know that you'll always be my best friend. I'll always have the memories, from kindergarten through senior year. I'll always have the scars from that one time we tried to climb that tree and failed. I'll always have the long walks, the sleepovers, the movie nights, and the talks that I couldn't have with anyone else.

I'll always remember the person who picked me up when I was down. If that's all I have left, then I guess that's enough.

Always here,
Mary, age 18

Dear Baben,

I wish you had been loved more by your first people, but I am glad that we adopted you. Mom is very sorry that she kicked you off the bed when

you tried to snuggle. You are the best brother
I could ever have.

Your loving brother,

Oscar, age 9

Note from parent: Just an FYI—this is a cat.

⌒

Dear Fatima,

I know you can't read this because you're a
horse, but you're an excellent one. You are a great
jumper and you'll always try your hardest not to
let me fall off. Even though you were frisky, I think
that you did great in the last horse show. I love
jumping over cross rails, cantering, and riding
through the woods with you. It is so fun it almost
makes me laugh every time. You are very gentle
and I'm so glad you're my horse. I don't think
I could find a better one.

From,

Olivia, age 12

⌒

Dear Clotilde,

I feel like I knew you even though we never
met. You died about one year before I met your

daughter, Misha. Maybe wherever you are you already know all about her, but maybe you don't and never will.

When I first saw her, Misha was a skinny fourteen-year-old who always carried a stack of notebooks containing her journals and her poems. Although I didn't usually teach freshmen, I had one class that year and she was in it. After the first few days of classes, she showed up during my prep period and offered me one of her notebooks to read.

That's how I found out that you had died of AIDS the year before, and that your husband had died of the same disease the year before that. This was the mid-'90s when an AIDS diagnosis was pretty much a death sentence. You were a nurse, so you must have known what to expect as your illness progressed. In spite of this awareness, you were a hero to your family and to anyone who knew your story. Little by little, I learned so much about you from Misha's writing and our long talks. You made sure that your girls would stay together, in a home in a good neighborhood with friends and relatives to keep tabs on them. I don't know all the details of their lives, but you somehow made sure they had enough.

You would have been so proud to see your oldest daughters when they came to parent conferences. They looked very serious and professional in their businesslike clothes. The questions they asked sounded rehearsed, but it was clear that they loved and cared for their little sister and meant to fulfill the role of parents as best they could.

Clotilde, somewhere along the line I started feeling a really strong connection with you. I felt so sorry that you were missing watching your lovely daughters become fine young women, sorry that you missed high school and college graduations, weddings and births. You have seven grandchildren now. I was and still am in awe of what you did to prepare your daughters for their lives after your death.

All your girls are doing well, Clotilde. I know they miss you, but you did your best for them and they know it.

Your friend, age 67

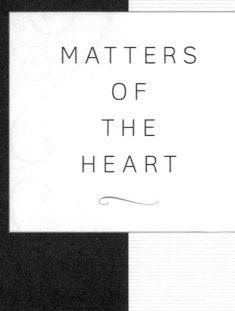

MATTERS
OF
THE
HEART

Ryan,

I cannot believe it has been so long. For some reason I woke up this morning and thought of you, something I don't think I have done in a while. I smiled and thought of how happy you would be to know I was going to have another baby, and thought wistfully of the two children of mine you have not met. I realized this morning that the anniversary of your passing was coming up soon, and then realized today was that day. It was hard to realize that. Five years. You would be thirty-one now, and you and Kim would be married, probably with at least a couple of children.

When you explained why you waited to propose to the love of your life until you were sure you were not going to be sent back to Iraq, I said I understood. I did, at the time. Waiting—putting things off—did not seem like a big deal. We were young and even the war could not get in the way of life. You were afraid of making her a "war widow."

On one hand, I am glad that you did not leave her a true widow, though I'm sure she was as married to you in her heart as she could ever be on paper. I am also glad you did not leave any babies without a dad. But, you missed that. In your efforts to spare someone you loved, you missed the chance to call her your wife and you missed the chance to hold your own babies. Now I don't wait for things anymore. I do understand that now is all we ever really have.

We spoke just days before you died (the only way a person should ever go, peacefully in their sleep), and we laughed and talked for the longest time. You were *so* happy. Life was just what you had always dreamed of and you deserved it. You spoke with so much excitement about your faith and your love of all those around you. I was, and still am, so happy for where you were and where I am sure you are now.

I used to tell myself (even though I knew it wasn't true) that maybe, just maybe, the marines made you fake your death so you could go back to Iraq on some super secret mission. Funny, I know. But you would have never gone for something like that. You would have never hurt your loved ones like that. So I know you're gone, I always have. But what I wouldn't give for that story to be true and to just run into you in some random place, or get some totally shocking crazy call from you and hear that hilarious laugh.

To have survived the war and come home and die doesn't make any sense to me at all. But maybe some people are just too good for this crappy world. You would definitely be one of them.

Love ya. Miss you.

C, age 32

Hello Christine,

I was thinking today that most men don't know how much they love their wives or girlfriends until after their wives or girlfriends walk out of our lives. Especially young men. I know it was that way for me. Of course, I wasn't that young age-wise, but I was blind when it came to my own emotions.

You and I have both moved on, but in the early morning hours, I still think of you. There are so many things I would say, if I could.

You were the only woman who I ever wanted to share my thoughts and feelings with, but again,

I didn't know it until after we divorced. Still that way today. When I see a sunset or a flower or think of something that is funny, I still find myself wanting to turn to you.

I miss you. Still do, even after twenty-three years. I never figured myself to be the kind of person who could love a woman for that long, especially a woman who doesn't love me back, but there it is. Go figure.

What would I have said? I love you, more than I know. I will wait for you, no matter how much time you need or what you decide. Before I met you, for many years, I would not let myself be involved with relationships because I knew that pain is the end result of relationships. And even though losing you was the worst pain I have ever felt, I would do it all again, if I could only hear you say I love you and see you smile at me again, if only for a day.

While my kids are the apple of my eye, I know the days would be sweeter, the world would look prettier, if you still loved me.

I am sorry I was such an emotional coward back then. I should have waited for you.

I have decided that I am not going to give up hope. I have lived without hope for many years, and it is a dark and lonely place to be. So, even if it's a one-in-a-billion shot, I have decided that living with hope, however small, is better than living with no hope at all.

Always yours,

Ray, age 59

My dearest beloved husband,

Throughout your eight-year cancer battle, you suffered greatly each and every day. Your courage, positive attitude, and will to live throughout your entire ordeal have inspired me to keep going, even when I no longer care to do so, over and over again. My grief is a constant companion. It doesn't seem any different to me now than it did in the weeks after you died. Sometimes I wonder if you can see me now and know how much I truly miss you.

The last time that I drove you to the ER, we were both quite upset. You said to me that you were sorry for all the travels we had taken, that we should have saved the money and then I would have been more financially secure after you were gone. I would not want to have a single penny in my bank account that we spent on those travels. I wouldn't be able to survive this time if it were not for these exquisite memories! We seized the day, carpe diem; we did not wait for our old age to travel, to seek adventure, to follow our passions. You would never have an old age, so how blessed were those decisions?

I hope you know, wherever you are, that your brave spirit lives on in my heart and will forever dwell there! I hope you know that I continue to put one foot in front of the other every day in honor of your struggle and love.

I will always be your devoted wife and caregiver and you will always be my beloved husband: my Tarzan, my Errol Flynn, my Neil Armstrong, my Jacques Cousteau, my Superman, the star of all my marvelous memories.

Gail, age 56

Dear Grandpa,

I'm sorry we never met, but I've heard a lot about you. I just want to tell you that he's okay.

That he's done well for himself. I know you've worried about how he'd be, how everyone in the family would be when you weren't around, but I need you to know this: he has taken care of them all. They're all doing their own thing and are happy. You'd be proud of him. I know I am. He's my dad.

All my love,
Meka, age 32

⌒

Dear Michael,

I had the biggest crush on you in fourth grade. I guess you liked me, too, because you came to school one day and gave me a little quartz crystal in a box. I was so shy that I don't think I ever thanked you, but I was so very touched.

We were in a brand-new classroom next to the auditorium and my heart was just bursting with love for you. I wrote your name very small in ink on a bare piece of wood on the door to express what I felt I could not say. Disaster struck the following day when the teacher and principal, both scary nuns, made you stand in class and accused you of the deed, though you staunchly denied it. Sitting next to you, I was so scared and shy I did not say it was me who wrote your name.

I felt like a traitor to you, feeling I had wronged you mightily, and have regretted it to this day. My shame further caused me to withdraw from you, and perhaps you thought it was because you were suspected of vandalism. I profusely apologize. I am so very sorry and regret my actions to this day. I almost threw away the crystal in shame more than once over the years, feeling I did not deserve it. Though it was nearly fifty years ago, I hope you can forgive me.

Much love,
Patty, age 57

Dear Connor,

I've been wanting to tell you how I feel, but I was afraid, and still am. Afraid of what to say, how to say it, when to say it, and what you'd say in return. One day I'll be able to, and hopefully spelling it out will help, so here it goes. You make everything better, you make me better, and I love you.

Yours,

Erin, age 25

~

Dear Kathy,

You asked me about what happened between your mom and I, but there was no way I would tell you. You are too young to understand how hard it was.

I cared about what you thought of me, and I loved you and your brother as my own. Everything I did was for your mom, you, and Brandon. I still feel sad that your mom didn't turn out to be the woman I was looking for. She wasn't the right one, and never will be. I had to leave, I needed to find someone else.

I miss you two deeply. I hope good things for you guys, always. I'll miss your laughter, the fun times, and the nice way that you were to me. I'll miss your birthdays. I'll always hope I see you again.

I'll never forget you, Kathy.

Al, age 42

Dear John,

When I first fell in love with you, I was fifteen. We dated three beautiful years. You crossed the country from Washington to West Virginia to be near me when my parents' divorce took me away from our home, but I soon felt we needed to grow up a little and so I felt I had to ask you for a break.

When you called me and told me about the new girl, when you asked me to help you pick out an outfit to wear on your first date—I died. I never believed it when people said that a broken heart could feel fatal, until then.

One February I visited home, and I visited you. We spent a long weekend reconnecting in all ways. It was clear that we were still deeply, deeply in love. We were closer to being back together than we had been in six years.

Now here I am, ten years later and still in love with you. I believed in us then and I believe in us still. I met a man and I fell in love with him, but it was never the same. I was always reserved, always waiting and hoping.

But now it's September. And this weekend you will marry the girl who isn't me. And my heart, for the second time, is shattered. And I don't know when it will be okay again. I have waited for you for ten years, John. I have waited and you have hurt me time and time again.

So, before it's too late, and for the last time, I wanted to ask you—please don't do this. Please don't marry her. You know that it's not what you want. Maybe it's what half of you wants but the other side knows it's wrong. Please, please, please just follow your soul—it will lead you to where it belongs. It will lead you to me.

Jess, age 25

⌒

Dear Baby,

I hope you know I love you. You live with wonderful parents right now who take care of you better than I ever could. I spent four days with you and they were the best of my life. I'm wondering if a day will come when you're eighteen and you'll want to meet me. I'm afraid of that day, afraid you won't want to, but I hope it comes. There was a

book my mother always read to me when I was
little and I want to convey one message to you:
"I'll love you forever, I'll like you for always, as
long as I'm living my baby you'll be."
Sarah, age 21

⁓

Dear World,

Can we please stop these senseless wars? I need
my soldier back so we can start our lives together.

Love,

Laura, age 21

⁓

Dear Samantha,

It has been seven years since I have seen you.
You must be, what, fourteen now? I have
wondered all these years what happened to you.
I have hoped and prayed that life has blessed you
abundantly. I want you to know that you left an
indelible print on my heart all those years ago when
I was your teacher. You changed my life forever.
There are tender thoughts that I need to share with
you that I couldn't say to you all those years ago.
You were too young to understand at the time.
And, well, I was too afraid to say the words to you.

Most days when you walked into my classroom, I inevitably would become frustrated with you over something. You were either arriving late to my class or never coming prepared with your homework, books or other needed supplies. You were a difficult child to teach because many things that were taught in my classroom did not come easy for you. You seemed so unsettled, so unfocused. Yet despite all of this, you always seemed to find happiness in things. Despite my nagging you about where your homework was or why you weren't paying attention, you did your best to keep a smile on your face and stay positive.

I still remember the day that you came up to my desk during recess when you had to stay inside to finish one of your many uncompleted and late assignments. I vividly remember the scowl on my face as you approached me and said, "Mrs. M . . . I am scared." I remember my heart softening a bit when I heard those words. I knew only a little about your home life, but not enough to prepare me for what you were about to tell me. I knew that you were living with foster parents. I also knew that you and your siblings had been split up. But that is about all I knew.

When you approached me that fateful day and told me you were scared, I was a bit taken aback. I immediately thought that I had done something to scare you, and I was so worried and concerned. And yes, I was quite humbled. I remember pulling you close to me, putting my arm around you and asking, "Sweetie, why are you scared?" And then you, this innocent, sweet spirit, looked into my eyes and shared with me the most heartbreaking account I had ever heard as a teacher.

You said, "Mrs. M., I am scared and don't want to go tomorrow." I asked you where you were going and you said, "To court . . . to see the judge." You continued, "I have to see my daddy and tell the judge what he did to me." You then pulled up your pant legs and showed me scarred legs from your ankles to your knees. Small, circular burn marks where your father, in a drug-induced rage, had taken his cigar to you (when you were just a baby) and burned you repeatedly by pressing his lit cigar into your tiny legs.

I still remember feeling the tears well up in my eyes and the pain in my heart as you shared your painful story. I remember you crying and telling me how much you missed your mommy and how you just wished you could go live with her. I remember feeling as if someone had hit me in the chest as I looked and felt the cigar burns on your legs. A feeling of helplessness washed over me because I didn't know how to make you feel better. But what I remember most is the awful guilt I felt for not being more intuitive to your needs. Angry and ashamed that I, as your teacher, had not sensed that there was a deeper reason for why you acted the way you did in my classroom. For there was no doubt, at the tender age of seven, that you were carrying the weight of the world on your shoulders. A burden that no seven-year-old should ever have to carry.

I still remember hugging you so tightly and rocking you that day in my class. It's all I knew to do. I wanted to take you home with me and care for you for the rest of your days.

What I want you to know, Samantha—what I need you to know—is that you changed my heart and mind forever that day. Not only as a teacher, but as a human being. You, Samantha, were the stepping-stone for preparing me to open my heart to the fact that I could love a child who was not from my own womb as if she were my own flesh and blood. You were an angel sent from above to prepare me to meet my beautiful son, Noah. You planted the seed for me to open my heart and home to other children like you who desperately want loving, stable, peaceful homes to grow up in.

I have prayed for you over the years. I continue to pray for you and hope that you have found a forever family that values you and loves you for the precious angel you are. I will be eternally grateful that you were put in my path in this life.

All my love,

Mrs. M., your second grade teacher, age 38

⌐∽

Steven,

I'm ready to say, "I love you."

Love,

Chelsey, age 18

⌐∽

Wife,

I don't know where to begin. I am so sorry for the past thirteen years. Things were good and then my world fell apart. I lost the business I had put everything into, hoping it would succeed so I could give you everything you wanted and, more importantly, deserved.

When I came home and told you it was done and I was terminated, your reaction hurt me then and still hurts me to this day. Your comments of "What did you do? You had to have done something wrong" put me on an emotional island and I have been struggling with that ever since. We have not shared a moment of intimacy since then and it doesn't seem to bother you at all. Perhaps we are nothing more than friends at this point, who share a house and occasionally socialize with our mutual friends.

I want so much more out of my life. I want someone to hold and love again. I want someone to come home to who will welcome me home with a smile. Someone who will make me want to succeed beyond my wildest expectations, like it was when we first met.

I don't know if we can ever get back to that point in our lives. Sometimes I wonder if we really ever had that type of relationship at all, or if I have been trying to convince myself of a relationship that really never got past the college "fun" stage and wound up in a marriage that shouldn't have been.

Either way, I realize that it is inside of me to change the way I feel and react to you. I am sorry for any suffering or unhappiness you have had because of me. I have decided to make a better, brighter future for myself. I am going to do whatever it takes to get back on track with my career. I hope you want to come along for the ride because it is going to be a great one.

Your husband, age 55

~

Dear Pancreatic Cancer:

I write to you as, again, you are trying to rear your evil head. This time, it is my mom you're trying for.

I am here to tell you that I am not that scared little girl I was back when you took my Pop Pop from me and I was too young to understand exactly what he went through or how to help in any way.

This time it is different. This time, I am prepared to face you and help my mom win this battle you placed her in. She is the best mom a girl could ask for. When I was young and sick myself, she took care of me, loved me, and nurtured me. When she was told that there was nothing that could be done for me, she fought for me and she was right.

Now I am older and wiser, healthy, and very willing to stand with her and fight the fight.

Nothing can stand up to a mother's love and a daughter's determination to help her. Someday you will no longer be able to hurt anyone again.

I hope you're ready, because we are not backing down.

Susan, age 43

⌒

Dear Cody,

I love you. You're the only man I've ever truly loved. You're not even close to the man of my dreams, you're ten thousand times better. I couldn't have dreamed you up. You are stand-up, honest, hardworking, loving, caring, funny, loud, obnoxious, carefree and

downright handsome. You are the perfect guy
for me.

So please take the hint of me moving
back home as I am ready to marry you.
Please ask me already. I've been waiting eight
long months. I've showed you pictures of
rings, brought up other people's weddings and
more. I know you well enough to know you've
always taken your sweet time and done things in
your own way. But please hurry! I don't want to
wait to be your wife. I love you. Always have,
always will.

With love,
Jade, age 19

Dear Grandfather,

I wish I could talk to you. You seem so great the
way my dad talked about you. I wish you hadn't
passed away by an accident. I wish I could ask
about your job as a police officer in Bangladesh.
You helped my dad be great. I will always
remember you.

Your grandchild,
Deepto, age 9

Dear Debbie,

I remember the first night that we met back in 1976. It was March sixteenth, a Tuesday night; my second night of work at my very first part-time job. When you came up to me to say hi, I went completely numb on the inside. Over the next couple of months we became best friends. I soon realized that I loved spending time with you. Even on days when I was feeling a bit down, knowing that we'd be hanging out later that day would change my whole demeanor. That's the effect you had on me. Before too long I knew that I couldn't ask you to be my girlfriend. As a growing and maturing young adult I was still learning how to interact in my relationships with the opposite sex. As a sixteen-year-old I was worried that if we did date, it could end in a breakup and the friendship that we so enjoyed together would end as well. I decided that I'd rather have you in my life long term as my friend than short term as my girlfriend.

The years went by and our interactions went in and out. My first marriage ended in divorce.

I know that subconsciously I tried to compare my wife to you, and therefore I never was happy in our marriage. I truly am sorry to my ex-wife for that. Thirty-some-odd years later and I find myself thinking about you every day.

Deb, I love you more today than ever before. I wonder how glorious my life would have been with you beside me. I know that I could have moved mountains because that's how you made me feel. But alas, I now fear that there is a very real possibility that you're not with us anymore. I have nightmares about something happening to you. Now all I'm left with are memories and they fade with time, too. But my love for you remains forever strong in my heart. And if you truly are no longer a part of this world, you will always be forever a part of me. Thank you for your love, your friendship and your grace. I am most certainly blessed.

All my love,
Randy, age 50

IF I
HAD
ANOTHER
CHANCE

Dear Ralph,

I miss you. You were a wonderful husband and even better father, and Emily misses you even more than I do. It's been twenty-three years, eleven months and fifteen days since you were killed in that car wreck and sometimes it feels like yesterday.

I really regret that I didn't laugh at all your jokes. You'd try to crack me up when we were arguing, when I was frustrated by life and bills and all the stupid little things that made me mad. You'd play the fool for me and I would withhold my laughter to punish you because of my bad mood. I should have laughed. I'm sorry.

Love forever,

Me, age 52

Dear little one,

It has been twenty-three years now and I still think about you all the time. Who you could have been. I am truly sorry for the life that you never got to have. The breath you never got to take. I was only fifteen and my mother made the decision for me. I really thought that I could have you and raise you, but I never really thought it all out. Even my best friend agreed that we could do this. But the nineteen-year-old boy that helped to create you never admitted that he was your father. No one really knew that it was him. And I was so naive. Didn't know how the world worked. I hate what we did—my mom and dad and I—but it was supposedly to save me from being a failure in my future life. So I could graduate high school, and maybe go to college.

You have three brothers now and a sister, too. Some of them know about you. The younger ones don't, of course. It's so hard to talk to anyone about you, without being so nonchalant about the whole thing. I try to let young girls know that it's not easy. And what a procedure like that does to a young girl's head. A child's head. It's something I live with every day of my life.

I will never see you. And I have no idea if you would have been a boy or a girl. But I want to ask that you forgive me for being an irresponsible kid. I do love you and I always think of you when people ask me how many kids I have. You come up more than I would have thought you would. I miss who you could have been. I really do.

Love, your mommy,
Alicia, age 39

⌒

Dear Grandma,

The day before your stroke, you drove me to the train station so I could spend the day downtown with my friends. You were always willing to drive me wherever I wanted to go. You would pull into the driveway, honk your horn once, and out I'd come ready to go. I'd sit down and look for whatever treat you had for me—a few homemade cookies, a cup of warm tea, a box of Cracker Jack. That day, since it was early, you had a banana and some juice ready for me. I took one sip of juice and complained that it tasted awful when it mixed with my toothpaste. I ignored the banana completely. You asked me what my plans were for downtown. Being fifteen and stupid, I gave you one-word answers: "stuff," "hanging out," "looking at things," "taking pictures." We got to the station where my friend was waiting. I practically clawed at the door to leave. You told me to stay safe, and that you loved me. I said, "Yeah. Bye." I rolled my eyes as I got out.

When the stroke took your body and your mind, we lost you. The words you say that even you know don't make sense and the things we all have to go through to make sure you stay safe are killing us all. We hate to see you this way. We hate knowing you're trapped in this shell of what you once were. I hate the fact that I can never tell you how sorry I am and have you recognize what I'm talking about.

I'll never forgive myself. I had a chance to enjoy a final ride with you. I had a woman in my life who cared for me unconditionally. I had a seventy-year-old woman who stood in the backyard with me so I could practice my softball pitch. I had a woman who would sit under the dining room table and play dolls, or let me mess up her hair in the name of my budding (albeit pretend) fashion salon.

All you ever did was care for me, and I wouldn't even say "I love you" back. And now, every single time I see you, I think about that day. And every single time I'm with you, I tell you I love you. Sometimes I get a "you too" in response.

Sometimes I don't. I know one day I'll never hear it again, but I promise that I will never stop saying it. I love you, Grandma. Thank you for everything you've done for me. Thank you for being wonderful. I miss you.

Your granddaughter, age 21

⌒

To the little girl at the cheerleading competition,

I'm sorry for hiding your bear under the bench. I only wanted to make friends with you, but didn't know how to ask you to be my friend. I wanted to give it back but then I didn't know how to go up to you and say, "Here is your bear that I hid." It was the right thing to do, but I was too embarrassed.

I made a huge mistake and I am sorry. I wish I didn't blow the chance to be your friend. You looked very kind and I know we would have been great friends. I wish you knew how bad I felt when I saw you look back. I would have been very upset, too, if a stranger took my bear and hid it. I hope one day I see you again.

From,

Sarah, age 10

⌒

Dear Mom,

It would have been so easy. I had won a free trip to Hawaii. I knew you would love to go. But I was busy with my own life as a single professional. There was time. I'd make the travel arrangements later.

One year later, you ran out of time. You died of a fast-moving cancer and I missed the chance. Losing you was so final. There's always another chance in life until you come to the end of it.

So now, I laugh loud. I tell my husband I love him. I take those trips. I go for that walk. I don't mind making mistakes for things I've done.

I just don't want to regret the things I didn't do.

I love you.

Glory, age 46

To my precious son,

Years have gone by since the divorce of your dad and I, yet I still feel regret and sadness in my heart at my choice of letting him keep you and raise you. You were only seven. A boy needs his mom and I let you down. I know you felt abandoned when I took your sister and moved several hours away. I can't even imagine how much pain and sadness you went through. I saw it affect you in your relationships as you got older. Never trusting. Your dad was the best dad for you, I know. But you needed me. And you needed your little sister, too. I can't believe after all these years, the tears still well up in my eyes at the thought of this. I know I was young myself—twenty-three when we got divorced—but that is of no comfort to me at the age of fifty-six. It was the worst decision of my life, and even though I have asked your forgiveness many times, I guess I have not forgiven myself.

You are now married and have a beautiful little son yourself. That little man will look up to you his whole life and I know you will never let him down. I feel really blessed that I can now be there for you and your family.

Your mom, age 56

To the girl in gym class,

In junior high, we stood beside each other every day in gym class. We waited for our names to be called and I would say "here," but you wouldn't. I thought it was because you were from India and couldn't speak our language, but I now know that isn't the reason. You would always smile and be shy, but you would sniff at us. Occasionally, we would laugh and make fun of you because of it. You wouldn't speak. I don't believe you even understood we treated you badly.

I regret that, every day of my life. If I cared at the time to know your name, I would look you up and apologize profusely. Not only because it is horrible to make fun of anyone that is different, but because I now know what made you different. The reason I know is because my son is an awful lot like you. He smiles a lot and is good-natured. He does things that I know, when he is older, kids will think are weird. I also know that he wouldn't understand if someone was making fun of him. He is autistic. When I heard that a symptom of autism is smelling people and things, my heart sunk. I remembered you. I wanted to cry. I didn't even know what autism was when I was twelve.

I have felt in the past that the reason my son is autistic is because of how I treated you. I hope that is not the case, but if it is, I atone for it every day. I atone as I watch my son's twin brother excel as he falls more and more behind. I atone when I keep trying new medical options and therapies and slowly become more bankrupt trying to find a cure. Autism has taught me to think twice before I judge, just as I should have done many years ago with you. I hope one day you can forgive me as I can never forgive myself.

Brittney, age 29

~

Dearest Emily,

You are gone now, up in heaven where you are able to play with your daddy. Please know that I loved you so very much, yet I didn't show it very well. I was never a good father to you or any of my human children. I was too obsessed with having a perfect yard to know what a great little girl that you are. I know that I had too much of a temper, but it was because I was too selfish to adequately show my love. I have learned, since you were gone, that I don't have my priorities right, and unfortunately I didn't realize it until after you were gone. I wish I was the person back then that I am now. I have done a lot of growing up since you passed away, and it was because of your death that I realized that I should have appreciated you more. You were a wonderful little girl, so full of happiness.

Jenna and Grandma got me a pretty decorative rock with your name on it, so I could put it in my backyard among the pretty flowers. Every time I see it, it makes me smile. I remember all of the times with you, from the day that Santa brought you to me on the night before Christmas, to the painful day that you went up to heaven. I am lucky enough to have your ashes in my favorite room, right next to your picture. I see it multiple times every day, and every time I smile, for God gave me a perfect little girl who helped me grow up. I am a different man now, and it's because of you that I have turned out to be a much more loving person. You taught me a lot. I just wish you were here so that I could show it to you now.

Grandma, Jenna and Matthew still talk about you, about how much they loved you and miss you still. And please know, not a day goes by that I don't think about you, miss you and love you. Keep running and chasing that ball, lay next to your papa, and know that you changed people's lives.

I love you forever,
Grandpa, age 47

～

Dear Mom and Dad,

Christmas is less than two weeks away and I know exactly what I want to give you both: the life we used to have. Every day I see the struggles that have been brought upon this family and I am deeply sorry for that. I understand and believe that everything happens for a reason, but if I could change what happened months ago, I would. Savannah could have waited for me. That trip was going to be perfect, when in reality, it just created a pain that was unknown in our family. The accident has changed all of our lives forever, especially both of yours.

Mom, I would give you all of your movement back and take away your wheelchair. If I couldn't do that, I would give you enough money for enough therapy to help make a true difference. And Dad, I would give you the power to never tire,

for you are always loving and looking after Mom,
never, ever complaining of the tasks at hand.
I'd give you both the money needed to renovate
the house to Mom's specific needs.

I really admire you both more than I have ever
let on and I apologize for never being more open
about my emotions and the pain this whole family
has experienced. I will admit, I have never
witnessed a greater love. I think that is truly
amazing and am so truly happy that you are my
parents. I just wanted to let you know how much
I truly love you both! I hope the pain is able to
diminish more and more each day.

Love,
Your daughter, age 18

Dear Melanie,

You were too young to die in the car accident—
so much ahead of you. Your wedding day was
approaching quickly, along with my grandchild
growing strong inside you. I'm so sorry that I cried
when you told me you were pregnant. I'm so sorry
I said, "You ruined your wedding!" I regret many
of my "parenting" moments but this one .s my

biggest. If only I would have been as happy as you were. If only I would have celebrated with you. If only you wouldn't have died. I'm so sorry. I love you and your unborn child who was never to see the world or be held by a judgmental grandmother. Please forgive me. I can't forgive myself.

Love you,
Mom, age 50

⁓

Jake,

When it came time to tell the truth, I let my anger and my pain get in the way of what I truly wanted. For almost ten years, you were my friend; someone I considered family and the man I thought I would marry. Our lives parted when you left to join the service. I was angry that you did not choose to stay with me. In time, I learned that fighting for your country was something you had to do, and I couldn't be angry at you for that.

For the next five years I waited, waited for the time to be right and for you to come back to me. While waiting, we planned our life together. We always found a way back to one another. The love in your face when I landed in Savannah is something I will never forget. The phone calls from overseas always made my face light up. Every time my phone rang with an unlisted number I would answer with the biggest smile on my face because I knew it was you. Those close to me knew that smile could only come from you; there was never a need to ask who had called.

As it approached the end of your contract, you told me you would not be coming home, and your future was to continue on the east coast while I remained on the west coast. I was hurt because once again you did not choose me. After nine years. I offered to sacrifice what was important to me if you would do the same later, and your answer was no. I was never upset at you for that, just hurt that I wasn't enough. So when you told me you never planned on coming home, I was distraught because I knew it was time to let go. So I did just that.

Within a month of letting go of a relationship that had meant so much to me, you changed your mind and came home. Just temporarily, but you finally came home. We never could decide at the same time that we were meant for one another. I was infuriated that you waited till I had let go. The months you were home, I just stayed away, angry. Instead of telling you why I hesitated, why I was upset, I told you that we could never be and that it was too late. That we both wanted different things. The truth is not that we wanted different things; we had been planning the details for years. Our values, our beliefs were all in line. I just wanted you to make some of the sacrifice I was willing to make for you. When you finally showed you would sacrifice for us, I protected my heart and lied.

There is not a day that goes by that I don't think about you and wish I could take back that day, take back my words and tell you the truth. The truth is that I love you, that I always will and that I would follow you around the world if that is what it took for us to be together.

I think you only fall in love the way we did once in a lifetime, that you can fall in love again but it is never quite the same. I know that I am too late and you have found new love. I hope that she treats you like the amazing man that you are and never misses an opportunity to tell you the truth.

Always and forever,

Kara, age 27

Dear Xavier,

I wanted to have you more than anything in this world. I feel as if you are now watching over me, but I can't forgive myself for rejecting a gift from God. You were due on my birthday, August thirteenth, and I had already imagined all of the fun things that we would do together. I just was so scared and had no support from anyone, especially your father. He was abusive to me and I feared that he would do the same to you, or worse, that you would grow up to be like him. I feared that, under the circumstances, you would not have received the love you deserved from me.

Still, that is not a justification for me getting rid of the very blessing that I had dreamed of for the last ten years. I cry every day wishing I could go back in time and change my decision. I still hear your heartbeat and remember the flickering on the monitor. I am now only the shell of the woman I used to be. A thousand times over I am so sorry and love you unconditionally. I hope that we will

one day meet in heaven, so long as God forgives
me for my sins.

Mom, age 27

⌒

Dear Prom Date,

I was your prom date for our senior prom. I am
so sorry for how I behaved that night. I wanted
so badly to go to the prom and you were the only
one who asked me, so I said yes. But I didn't want
to be there with you. I wanted to be there with
someone popular. I remember I ditched you at one
of the after parties, although you found me again
at the breakfast and drove me home. I hardly
spoke to you. It has been thirty-three years and it
still upsets me when I think about it. I am so
ashamed.

I wish I had been nicer. I wish I had enjoyed the
evening with you. I am sorry I ruined your night.

A few years ago, I was at the holiday party for
my husband's company and his new director came
and sat with us at our table. I found out he is your
brother-in-law. It brought it all rushing back to
me, the shame. My husband was laid off a month

later and I have always wondered if it was because of that conversation.

I hope you have found happiness in your life.

Vicki, age 50

~

Dear Mom,

I wish I told you how much I admired your huge heart and capacity for love by adopting five children from Korea, Germany, and the U.S. Although none of us looked alike, there was never a doubt in my mind that I was yours. I wish I told you how unfair it was that you got sick. I wish I listened to you as you were dying, needing to get your last thoughts out and instructions to me for after you were gone. I wish I told you that it was okay to live without the tubes that were keeping you alive instead of yelling and crying about you giving up. I wish I told you I love you more often.

Your loving daughter,

Ruth, age 50

~

Dear Baby Devin,

I only got to hold you twice. And you wiggled so much those two times that I called you Wiggle

Worm. I wish you could've stayed longer, but I think that if you had, you would have been so ill. You were already having so much trouble and I think God knew you would be better off staying with Him, so he picked you up and carried you away. From all of us. From your mom and dad, brothers, grandparents, aunts, uncles, cousins. We all miss you so terribly.

I kissed the dirt on your grave a few weeks ago. Every time I go to the cemetery, I visit you and all of the other little ones that are buried there. It still seems so unreal. All of it. It just seems like a terrible nightmare. And I can't imagine how your parents feel. I'm only your cousin and I cried every day for a week or two. Sitting in the shower asking God why he would take such a sweet baby. I wish that I could hold you again, but I wish more that your brother, Caleb, could hold you. The first time he got to hold you was when he carried your casket to the grave. I wish Granny could hold you. She misses you so. I wish your mommy and daddy could hold you. I wish I didn't have to write a poem in memory of you.

If I could see you one more time, I would tell you I love you and let everyone in your family hold, kiss, and love you. It's already been three months, but it still doesn't seem real.

All my love,

Lauren, age 20

Dear Grandma,

I wish I could have a little time with you. All I know is that your name is Sandy and that you died of cancer. In my world, you would be the best grandma ever. I know that you can't control when you die or not—it's not your fault. I wish I could go back in time and see you face-to-face, and I wish that I could know everything about you. I am grateful that you left me with a great dad.

Your grandson,

Austin, age 10

Hi Norman,

I was so shocked that morning in 1966 when the school announced that you had been killed walking to school by a hit-and-run driver. A few days earlier I had been the lighting director for our school talent show. Your act as a calypso dancer brought many looks and comments from the audience, along with a lot of ridicule. I felt so bad that I, too, had laughed and made fun of your act along with lots of others. Your full costume with the tight black pants, gaucho waistcoat, and a hat with tassels was a strange sight indeed.

You danced with such vigor and talent. Unfortunately that was overlooked. People were merciless to you in the following days, calling you such bad names. It was embarrassing to hear, but I did nothing to stop it or protect you. You were in my homeroom and there was some of the worst. Your sexuality was questioned along with your parentage. I did not see you retaliate at all. I did talk to my dad about the whole situation but still did not come forward.

Here it is, forty-three years later, and I still think about what I did not do. I guess it makes it worse when I cannot be sure if you were killed by one of our classmates that was still making fun of you. I can just see someone playing

chicken with you and it getting out of hand.
After all, you were just walking, and the reports
say you flew almost sixty feet in the air. The whole
school attitude changed after the incident, but no
one bragged or ever came forward to take
responsibility.

I can only pray that I can finally get to ask you
what happened when we meet in heaven. I hope
you have forgiven me for not coming forward and
protecting you. After all, I was the big jock who
could control a lot of the crowd that was terrible to
you. I know that I am a better person today from
the lesson I learned but still wish I had done better
when I was seventeen years old. I am now almost
sixty and you never got to see your eighteenth
birthday. I wish I could have told you this to
your face.

God be with you, Norm. I hope and pray
this letter may give me even more peace and
understanding and a better insight as to what
to do with the rest of my life.

Sincerely,

Tom, age 60

To My Younger Self,

I'm going to tell you something I'm sure you don't want to hear right now, but it has the potential to help you do something important. There are many ills that befall us in this life, and most we can't avoid, but this one you can.

I know how much you love summer camp, how much you look forward to it every year. Even at this advanced age, some of my best memories still come from there. Yet there are some facts you need to know.

This summer, there will be a counselor there who is a child molester. He is going to try to kiss you, and to make you do other things with him that you don't want to do. And he will do it repeatedly. I know you have been taught to be a good girl, and you believe that if you disobey him you will get kicked out of camp and will never be allowed to come back. I am writing this letter to tell you it is not true.

Although it is true that most of the time you should obey people in authority, sometimes people in positions of authority do bad things. Nobody has the right to kiss you or touch you in ways you don't want. Nobody has the right to make you touch them in ways you don't want.

So when this man tries to kiss you, run away. You know and trust the camp director's wife. Tell her what this man tried to do, and tell her you don't want him near you. She will listen to you, and he will be the one who will be told to leave camp and to never come back, because he is the one doing something wrong, not you.

I know this is true, because even if you don't speak up, three weeks later he will be thrown out of camp for doing the same things to another girl. Only by then you and she will have suffered a long-term hurt that could have been avoided if only you had known you have the right to defend yourself.

So when the time comes, run, and speak up, and know it will be just the first of many brave acts yet to come.

Susan, age 46

UNFINISHED
BUSINESS

～

Dad,

I can't begin to tell you how many feelings I go through in one day, even in one hour. I tend to be angry, sad, happy, enraged, content, accepting, and emotionally void all throughout one point in time. I catch myself zoning off into space while driving or trying to focus on school or work. I don't know why you chose to leave us that day. What could have been so bad that you decided to end your life?

I saw you three days earlier and invited you to Christmas. I waited around all day so I wouldn't miss your visit. I talked to you for an hour at the table and helped you find apartments. I tried to reassure you that everything was going to be okay. I showed you my support. You gladly accepted the Christmas invitation, smiled, and even began joking with me. I felt like things were getting back on the right track and that we would be able to be a communicative family again after enduring two long months of horrible fighting between you and Mom, two months which led to your separation.

You told me to go food shopping and told me that you needed to talk to Mom, alone. I obeyed you, gave you a hug, said good-bye, and went shopping. I don't know what you and Mom talked about that day and I guess I never will. Maybe you pleaded for her to get back with you and she declined. Maybe you were talking about finances, maybe she revealed a secret, I don't know.

I answered the house phone that night when you got back to your brother's house, and you said you were home safely. We chatted for a few minutes and then hung up. If I had known that was the last conversation that I was ever going to have with you, I would have made it much more meaningful. I didn't hear anything in your tone that would have convinced me otherwise; I believed that you were going to be okay.

When I was unable to reach you two days later, I just had this gut feeling that you were gone. Your phone was off and you weren't answering e-mails and no one could find you. It was then that I knew. My life has fallen apart since that day that you left me. I'm trying to pick up the pieces but it's an hour-to-hour process. Thanksgiving, the anniversary of your death, and Christmas are all coming up, and I don't know how I'm going to make it through. I've grieved so much in these past eleven months and I don't know what I have left in me.

This letter is a jumble, but sadly, that is my life lately. I can't seem to make sense of anything. I go over those last few days time and time again, trying to retrace my steps and see if there was anything that I had done. I blame myself for your death. I know I shouldn't, but I do. I feel like you were thinking of something I said to you when you did it. What if my actions or my words led to your choice? I wish you could send me some kind of sign to let me know that you're still around because I simply don't feel your presence anymore. I feel like you hate me and it was my fault and that's why I don't feel you around. I can't believe I have to live an entire lifetime before I meet you again and get the answers to all of my unanswered questions. It just seems like a long time for a daughter to live without her dad. Words cannot explain the amount of pain I am feeling and how apologetic I really am. I guess it never dawned on me that a dad would willingly choose to leave his daughter. I always thought you would be here to walk me down the aisle and hold my firstborn. Looks like that day will never come.

Missing you deeply,
Your daughter, age 23

~

To my little sister,

I know you probably hate me for all of the pain I put you through. The hitting, screaming, calling you mean names, and being mean. I know that I am not the best sister the world could give you, but please understand. I hate to say this but I have been jealous of you since you were born. You were always the apple of Mom's eye. Never once have I heard "Good job!" or "Wow, that's really good" or "You're so smart." It hurts me to no end and soon my hurt and sorrow turn into rage. I know I'll never be looked at like I am unique and special. So be happy that you are loved in such a way, even if it hurts me.

Your sister, age 18

Dear Grandpa and Grandma,

I wish we could meet each other. I can only imagine what fun we could share going to football games, the zoo or the movie theater. My number one goal in life is that I live to meet you before it's too late. I feel as if there is a hole in my heart when I think about you. I would give up all my belongings just for a day with you. I can almost hear your voice in my head.

With love,

Joel, age 10

Dear Mom,

It's been almost a year now. I know I must have surprised you when I moved away and stopped answering your calls. I've felt so trapped in a life that I didn't want, a life that you gave to me. Ever since I was a little girl you dressed me up, put me on diets, and did my makeup. You treated me more like a doll than a child. I used to think that I was too fat or ugly to deserve the things I wanted in life. I've struggled with this notion longer than

you can even imagine. Even after therapy,
my self-image issues surface, especially
when I'm around other beautiful women. You
passed a heavy burden into my life that I don't
want.

I can't look at other beautiful women without
tearing them down in my head. I can't look at food
without feeling guilty. Even now, it's still difficult
to let my own friends see me without makeup.
I feel like I'm trying to live up to an unrealistic
expectation of beauty that doesn't exist. It's been
rough, but every day I get stronger. My life
improves because I'm learning how to be happy on
the inside. I wish you knew how to be happy
without your vanity. You didn't need the face-lift,
boob job, or lip injections. You could have also
done without that nasty anorexia. I wish you
could see an inner beauty in yourself that I'm
starting to see inside myself. I am beautiful, Mom,
no matter what you say.

From,

Kelley, age 19

Jonah,

First let me say, I love you. I love you more than anything in this life. I'm a terrible mom, Jones. I've let you down more times than I can count. I let you down when I chose drugs over you and had to go to rehab for nine months. You turned three while I was in rehab and I'll never forget the picture your Nana sent me in the mail of you crying. I'm sorry for moving you around so much because I couldn't hold down a job. I'm sorry for marrying the wrong man because I thought you needed a daddy. I'm sorry you had to see the divorce.

I'm sorry for working six days a week at a horrible job and not being able to spend more time with you. If you only knew how much I miss you throughout the day. I'm sorry I only read to you when I have to sign a piece of paper saying we did it. I should read to you every night. I'm sorry you used to sit at the dinner table to eat by yourself while I was in the living room watching TV. I'm sorry I make up excuses. There are plenty I have given you.

I'm sorry I don't put you first. I'm sorry that you don't have a father in your life. I'm sorry I moved you to a town where you had no friends and I never taught you how to go out and make new ones. I'm sorry I didn't have the money to take you somewhere cool over the summer break. I'm sorry that you don't believe in God because Sundays are my only day off and I'm too lazy to get up and take you to church.

Even though you are only eight and these things are adult problems, I know you see them and your life is forever changed by my mistakes and choices. I am so sorry, Jones.

Love,
Mom, age 31

Susan,

Please stay.

Love,
Rich, age 55

Matthew,

Your death was so sudden. You just went to sleep and didn't wake up. You were only nineteen. I miss you very much. This is your birthday month. You told me of all your dreams and what you wanted to become in the years ahead. You had a goal of joining the Peace Corps. You were such a caring person. You were always there when your mother needed help. You helped care for your younger brothers and spent many hours trying to tease your older brother.

I remember your smile and the twinkle in your eye. You were so artistic, and a wonderful musician. Animals loved you and you always had a cat or two around you. Your whole short life was a very difficult one, and a constant struggle due to poverty and problems at home. Grandmothers are not supposed to outlive their grandsons.

You are always in my heart.

I love you,

Grandma, age 67

⌒

Dear Uncle Mark,

I'm sitting in your old kitchen right now, babysitting your youngest son. He turned one this year, and I have been chasing him around the house while he bubbles with laughter. He looks so much like you, Uncle Mark, like a little clone of you. I know every time my father sees his nephew, your son, it's painful for him. You were his baby brother.

I remember the Saturday in Rome when his life fell apart, Uncle Mark. When the hotel phone rang, how was I supposed to know that giving the phone to my father was the worst thing I could do to him? How was I supposed to know my stepmom was going to tell him how you stood in front of the train the night before? The sun was rising on the beautiful streets of Rome and I wanted to wire explosives down every street. I wanted to turn the obliteration of my dad's life into something visual.

I hear you left a note, Uncle Mark. I don't know if I'm ready to read it.

Love,
Your only niece, age 18

⌒

Dear girl,

I don't know your name. Isn't that sad? To me, you have no name, no face, no physical structure. I have never seen you, and will never get to meet you. You are my late uncle's daughter; I am your younger cousin.

Your mother, whom I also don't know, was impregnated by my uncle Robert. After my uncle's tragic death, she came forward to inform my grandmother that she was pregnant, and that she was going to let another man claim you as his, to raise you into his family, and to give you his last name. She said she never wanted anything to do with us, and didn't want you to have anything to do with us, either.

I never met my uncle because he died before I was born. People say I look a lot like him, which leads me to wonder, do you look like me?

I'm not sure if my grandpa knows about you or not. He took your biological father's death very badly—they all did. You have three uncles and an aunt, and cousins, cousins, and more cousins. You have a big, loving, tight-knit family— which makes this all the more hard to write. To know that you are out there, and that you will never get to meet your adoring grandparents, your loving family.

I wonder how your life has treated you. Are you happy? Did they treat you well, and did your grandparents give you ice cream when you came to visit them like mine did? Do people often tell you that you don't look anything like your dad's side of the family? I wonder these things a lot, and it's hard to tell my fiancé about you when I don't know anything about you.

I wish you well in life, and I wish that you could meet our now-aged grandparents. Maybe you could have fixed the hole in my grandpa's heart after Robert died—he would have had something of his to hold on to.

Much love from your father's family,
Day, age 18

Dear Grandpa,

I hope you are doing well wherever you are, hopefully someplace wonderful. You've been gone for about seven or eight years and I can still remember the smell of your house, always filled with dinner aromas and warm hugs. Remember that one day that I was in the pool with Kasey and you told me that you wanted me to have your house later on down the road? I replied with "Grandpa, I don't want your house," because I was only a kid and didn't understand.

Now I wonder if you really thought that I didn't want your house. I really wish that I did have it because you built it with your own hands and no power tools. I also wonder if you did put it in your will for me but your children didn't want me to have it. Well, Grandpa, you would have been disappointed in them because they sold it. Now some strangers live in it. I think about it all the time. How I would have preserved it in your memory and made it just as you left it. I rarely drive by, but if I get the chance and I am around the neighborhood, I look at it and it makes me cry every time. It's not that yellow mustard color anymore and the shrubs that you loved to trim are almost all ripped out. If I had been older, I would have stepped up. You built it by yourself, with a hammer and nails, and no one seems to care but me. If I get the chance when I am older, I will go and buy it. I loved that house more than any house

I've ever been in and it belongs in our family. I just thought you should know that I really did care about your things.

I also wonder what happened to your precious-metal-detecting treasures. I ask my dad and other children of yours and no one seems to know. You had beautiful rings and little trinkets that you knew I adored so much. You told me that when I was older, the wedding ring you found could be mine. I wish it would have come true. I do not own anything of yours, Grandpa, and it makes me sad because all I have are memories. I am not a materialistic girl, but it would be really nice to have something of yours.

I will miss you every day for the rest of my life and I hope that if you are watching you are proud of me. I love you oodles and oodles, as you'd say. See you in my dreams.

Kylie, age 20

Dear Uncle Eric,

Why did you tear our family apart? There are many times I wish I could talk to you about how

I feel, but you won't let me. I wish we could be a family again. Now that you have decided not to have anything to do with us, the family has been left incomplete.

I remember the time my cousins and I accidentally sprayed a police car with the hose. When the policeman knocked on the door to discuss what we had done, we hid in the hay barn as you opened the door. I remember your deep voice calling our names. Though you were mad, I still could hear a hint of love slicing through the anger. I miss it. I miss your voice. I miss you. I miss the kind of family we used to be. Why did things have to change?

Your niece,
Rachael, age 11

Grandpa,

The last thing I said to you was "I hate you." The same words that have sunk deep inside of me for so many years now. Little did I know, that night you drove away would be the last time I would ever see you. That I would never get to wrap my arms around you, call you when something exciting happened in my life, or even just stop by and say hi. You were an amazing man who I miss dearly. You haven't missed much. I graduate in June and head off to a big university on a golf scholarship. You always knew I was meant to get out of this small town; I was just too stubborn to ever listen to you. Looks like you were right after all.

Mom and Dad are good; Mom just graduated nursing school and got a job at a new hospital. Dad has his own business now, something he never thought would happen. Both of them are working so hard. You'd be proud of them.

I miss our talks under the big oak in the middle of summer, hearing all of the stories from when you were growing up. Those are the memories I miss the most. You changed my life in so many ways. The night you got in that car and never came back was the night that I said those terrible last words to you. You probably died with bitter thoughts. I wish I could tell you in person how sorry I was for the things I said. Instead of having happy thoughts on that dreadful night, your head was filled with sorrow and despair. I want to take back that night and the screaming and yelling. Everything that was said that night. I'm sorry.

So many times I wish I could take it back or start over. There's not a day that goes by that I don't think about you. You're a loved man no matter how thickheaded you are.

Your granddaughter,

Ashley, age 17

⌒

Dear Wayne,

What you did all those years ago has colored my life every single day since, from the moment I found you on the floor of the shed, blood everywhere. To this very day, my life was irrevocably changed by your actions. I understand now that you were sick, but it doesn't really make things much better knowing that. There is not a day that I don't think about what happened or see it in my mind. I've learned to live with the pain, but not all that well. I still feel isolated from people. It's affected my health, too. I've never remarried, although I would like to have someone who would love me and be there for me and help me put this burden down. I want to live a life where I feel loved and valued.

Your mother was devastated and died much sooner than she would have if this had never happened. Your brother is left alone now. I know you weren't thinking about all of these things that night you put the gun to your head. But I sure as hell wish you had. I hope you are at peace. And I hope one day to find some.

Erin, age 49

Dear Dad,

Thanks for the harsh criticisms as a kid. Thanks for making me mold myself into a hardworking person who won't settle for anything less than best. Thanks for the constant reminder that money isn't the key to happiness and that you're nothing without your family behind you.

But after all of that, you could have done me a solid. You could have been faithful. You could have lived up to your own standards. I keep trying to advocate for you but I've realized I'm in denial;

you're just an asshole. I've got a list of issues to fix because of you.

I give up. I choose Mom.

Your daughter, age 20

~

Dear Stepmonster,

I hate that you don't have a job. I hate that all you do is work out, diet, and go to the stables to help disabled children ride horses because it "makes you feel good to give back."

I hate that you married my dad. I'd spend so much more time with him if it weren't for you.

I hate that he won't leave you. I hate that he's so afraid of being alone.

I hate that he keeps buying you shiny new cars when you crash them from driving drunk. I hate that you got your license taken away last year, and that now he has to drive you around.

Remember that night when you got really drunk and started throwing things? And Dad told me to go into the RV and watch TV until I fell asleep while he tried to deal with you? Remember how he eventually had to call the cops?

Remember that time a couple of years later when Dad was out for the day, and you started saying things to me that were so nasty and hurtful that I locked myself in the bathroom until he got home that night?

Remember when I came down for spring break a few years ago and you started arguing with me and got so violent that Dad and I had to spend the whole week at my grandparents' condo?

I didn't get to have a normal childhood because of you. I had to grow up so fast. I've dealt with things that children should never have to. You really have been the evil stepmother, like in the fairy tales.

I'd like to have my daddy back.

Sincerely,

Your stepdaughter, age 18

~

Dear Teej,

If I had known as the naive sixteen-year-old girl I was back when you took your life how fragile our hearts and minds really are, I would never have let you be alone for a second. If I had known the pain that this would cause me years later,

I would have told you I loved you. If I had known how it would tear apart your family, I would have done anything I could have. I can't imagine the pain you feel as you look down on us living our lives without you.

If I had known how tormented your mind truly was, I would have shut up with every trivial minor issue that I had. I would never have wasted your time with my silly problems that I so needed you to help me with. I wouldn't have been with Dan. I would have been with you. I love and miss you so much but at the same time, I'm so angry with you. I feel physically sick when I step outside my house and look across the water we used to see together. I no longer find relaxation in viewing the ocean on the rocks near our home. I no longer find solace in going for a walk because I have to walk by your godforsaken house that you killed yourself in. I can't look on your street without seeing ambulances and tears. I can't drive by the police station without remembering how it felt to be accused of supplying you with the drugs you killed yourself with. I can't cry anymore if I tried.

I'm twenty years old now. Four years have passed since I saw your body bag outside. Four years have passed since I first began the emotional torment I give myself for not doing anything. I'm growing up now. I'm in college and I'm working on my prelaw degree. I work really hard in all my classes and I have a few friends. I have a boyfriend, and it's not you. It's not anyone like you. I don't know if that makes it better or worse.

Sometimes I feel you helping me. One time, I lit candles in your honor on the ocean on your birthday, and when the waves went over the candles, they didn't go out. I swear they stayed lit. You were there that one time. Where were you the other times I could have used a loving presence?

I have a future now without you. I will never be able to explain to anyone how it feels that you are not here, and that I could have made a difference and had you here with me. I can't listen to any music that reminds me of you without feeling ill. I can't go through my day like a regular young woman without having the constant reminder of what you did.

I'm going to keep living and growing and getting further in life. I can only wish you would be here with me. I can only wish that this never happens to someone I care about. Did you know my mother told me no one will ever love me because I have your initials tattooed on my ankle? It's a constant reminder of the one person that supposedly did love me, as well as a notice that no one ever will come close to you.

I love you and I miss you but I can never forgive you,

Rsl, age 20

Dear Mom,

I haven't talked to you in forty-six years. You could say it sounds like forever, but it seems like yesterday when you dropped me off at the babysitter's, promising to return. I have always thought about what I would say to you and how I would say it. I'm not sure what that would look like, but it sounds sad. You never know, maybe I would laugh when I hear the story of why you didn't come back for your five-year-old child. Maybe you got arrested or maybe you met a really nice guy and he took you out to lunch. I do have to say that was a very long lunch. I think we would have had fun together. I became one of the best amateur fighters at 106 pounds in the country. You would have been proud. Although, after I retired from the sport, I got addicted to drugs and did fourteen years in prison. I sure could have used a good talkin'-to from you at that time. It seems all my relationships with girls are terrible. For some reason, I just don't trust the ladies. Anyway, you should stop by sometime and say hi.

Your boy,
Dave, age 51

Dear Nicole,

I've already written you a few things. I still haven't sorted everything out that I'm thinking and feeling right now, because you just died three days ago. So I apologize for the rambling, but you know how I am.

The main thing is . . . I'm so mad at you. I'm so mad that you didn't call me or Carrie after your car accident. And I know why you didn't call—you knew we'd make you go to the hospital. But you

were too tough. You didn't need help. You were
fine. And sure, you were a strong chick. But you
wouldn't ever ask for help, no matter how much
you needed it, and that may ultimately be why
you died.

I'm mad because it didn't have to end this way.
I'm mad that you knew how much I cared about
you, but you pushed me away anyways, in your
guardedness. And I'm mad at myself. I should have
just gone ahead and bothered you all the time
anyways, just to make sure everything was okay.
Maybe I didn't make it clear enough how much
you meant to me. Not many people knew the real
you. I wish that hadn't been the case. Not many
people knew how sad you were, how scared, how
lonely. You never said you were, but I know you
were. I'm sorry for that. I'm sorry I wasn't there for
you more, and sorry that I got so caught up in my
own life that I just assumed you'd be okay, and
that you'd be here forever. Because obviously,
I was wrong.

So now your girls don't have their mommy.
I feel the worst for them, especially your baby girl.
I hope that whoever ends up with her makes sure

she knows how special she is. I hope they love her as much as you did.

It's times like this I wish I believed that you were still around somewhere, that you could hear me, or see these words. I wish I believed that you're in a better place, because I think that might make this easier. Nevertheless, I find myself talking to you anyways. For some reason, almost every time I go in the bathroom, I start talking to you. Maybe because it's quiet and private in there, and I don't feel as silly betraying my lack of belief. I keep going back to look at your pictures. I look at your last post on Facebook, watching the time since you wrote it slip away, panicking at the thought of your last minutes getting further away from me. Like if I could just stop time from moving, I could go back and stop this from happening. But time continues to go by, and your death just gets more real, and it gets harder.

I am dreading your funeral next week. I know how these things go. You won't look right. I wish they'd let me fix your hair one last time, but then again, maybe that's not such a good idea. I know seeing you, lying there in your casket, is gonna make it all hit home. How can you really be gone? How did this happen? Twenty-seven isn't old enough to die.

I think about your last moments, and wonder if you knew what was happening. If you knew the end was coming. Was it painful? Were you scared? God, I hope not. The saddest part for me, though, is knowing that you were alone. I wish I could have been there, if not to help you, then to at least let you know that you were never alone. You were always in my thoughts, and you will continue to be, for the rest of my life.

I love you, girly.

Your friend,

Ursula, age 27

WHAT
I MISS
THE
MOST

Dear Ashley,

I wish you hadn't moved away. I never got to tell you how much I loved it when you played the violin. It was so much better than my piano playing. You were like an older sister to me. But one that never got cranky and always cared.

Remember that friendship bracelet you gave me? I do, too. Even though it is too small for my wrist, I wear it as a ring. When my mom told me that you cut your hair, I wanted mine short, too. It's still too short to put up in a ponytail. Is yours still short, too?

I wish you were still here to play with me when the boys play outside. Now I have to ride bikes with some obnoxious, weird, nose-picking boys.

I wish you never moved away.

Your friend forever,
Clare, age 11

⁓

Dear Dad,

I was only fifteen years old when you passed away at the young age of forty-two. I missed you so much, and even though it's been thirty-five years, it still feels like yesterday. I think it affected me more than my brothers and mom because we were so close. Mom was the disciplinarian and you were my hero.

I will never forget so many of the things that you did. First and foremost, you were a family man who loved us very much. I have never been able to find one like you. Do you remember when your buddies and you went fishing overnight? You came home at two in the morning because they were on the boat drinking. You woke us all up and took us to Shoney's in our pj's. That was so much fun.

I recall how, one morning, we got into this big fight. You checked me out of school to apologize to me. That was one thing I admired so much about you. You always owned up to your mistakes. One of the last things I remember was when you were sick and had to go to the hospital, which would be the last time you were at home. I was having Frosted Flakes for breakfast and you looked at them and said, "I wish I could have some of that." I told you not to worry, that you'd have them one day. That one day never came. You were gone ten days later.

Mom remarried four years later but he was not anything like the man you were. He was kind to her, but I always felt he would rather not have had to put up with "her kids."

I am sorry I didn't have the chance to tell you how much I love you. Thank you for being my dad.

Your daughter,

Tami, age 49

Dear Goldy,

I miss you so much that my mom had to buy me a bird and a dog. You assisted me. You were so unselfish. I wonder how you are doing. You were proficient at tricks.

Love,

Trenton, age 8

Dear Cory,

It's been one month and ten days since you died. I think about you every day. Every time I watch my daughter play with her little brother I think of you. There are so many things I wish I could tell you.

I want to tell you that I'm sorry. I'm sorry you were alone when your heart stopped and your car went off the road. I'm sorry that you were a John Doe when the paramedics couldn't find ID. I'm sorry you were alone in the ER for so long while your wife frantically called 911 to find out why her husband wasn't home yet. I'm sorry that I couldn't visit you more often after your accident. I'm sorry that you missed the birth of your second little boy (he's seven months old now, and a real cutie). I'm sorry you will never meet your newest niece (Mom told me she was born with just as much hair as you were). I'm sorry that I wasn't there when you breathed for the last time.

I want you to know that I am proud of you. You may have been young, but you were a wonderful brother, son, father, husband. You packed a full life into your short years, and I will always admire that. I will always be inspired by how hard you fought after the accident, first to come out of the coma, then to let us know that you were still there even though your body wouldn't move. I cried watching the video of you sitting and then standing in physical therapy. I haven't been able to watch it since you left us.

I feel cheated. We were robbed. Your life ended three weeks before your twenty-fifth birthday. You were too young. We were supposed to grow old together. We were a team: me, you and Kyle—siblings and friends forever. Now Kyle and I are left alone, and we're not quite sure how we'll manage without you in the middle. Kyle was the best man at your wedding, but you won't be here for his. It hurts more than I can say to know that your baby will have no memories of you.

Cory, I will always remember you as a loving, giving, occasionally annoying and exasperating younger brother. I will tell your sons stories about what you were like as a child and how much you loved them. I will tell my children about their uncle Cory—how special he was, and how much I loved him.

I will tell them that you started calling me "Spartacus" because I mentioned wanting a nickname and that was the most annoying one you could think of. I resisted for a long time,

but eventually I gave in and started answering
to it. I'm getting a Roman gladiator helmet
tattooed on my wrist. Every time I look at it, I will
remember you and how much I wish I could hear
your voice calling me "Spartacus" just one
more time.

I will love you forever,
Tiffany, your big sister, age 26

~

Dear Webb,

Our life was exceptional. You were my soul
mate, my friend, my husband, and a loving,
devoted father to our son. We never were short of
expression. Our affection, our mutual hobbies, our
desire to move mountains.

You were a man of thought, and of
consequence. You were determined to resolve the
world of its angst—many in your field admired you
as well as respected you, and many stood in line to
participate in your dream.

I miss my life with you. I miss our friendship
and the greatness in our marriage, which seemed
to encompass everything I do. I miss hearing you
call my name. I miss waking to you every

morning. There was nothing I needed to say because we were never short with our admiration for one another, or praise for a good deed accomplished, or a show of affection. We were always there for one another.

Your sudden demise shook our world with shock, dismay, depression and longing. I haven't been able to feel as much hope for life as when we were together. To this day, I continue to live in memory and agonize over each new day without your presence.

I just wanted you to know that I miss you, love you to this day, and that fondness continues to grow. I carry you in my heart and thoughts every day. I remain your wife, as I consider you still my husband, friend and father to our son. I wish I could turn the clock back and had the insight to understand what type of treatment was being administered, and had the education to know it was the wrong diagnosis. You would still be with me today, if I had known.

Love you, miss you.

Your wife,

Lys, age 54

Bullet,

It has been two months since I had to put you down and I am so sorry that it had to come to that. I have never felt so much guilt about doing something in my life. I wish I had done so many things different so that you might still be here with me. I replay that morning over in my mind, thinking how things might have been different if I would have held on to your leash tighter or taken you out later. You were truly the best dog. I wish we could have gone on one last run together or I could have given you once last ice cube. A little part of me died with you that day and I miss you so much. Please know that I love you with all my heart. You were not only my dog, but truly one of my best companions.

Scott, age 33

Dear Grandpa Dave,

If I could have a moment with you, I would want to hear you laugh one more time, smile again, and watch you ride off on your motorcycle just once more. I still wish today that I had asked you about your childhood and why you loved the things that you did. I would give just about anything to see you whip out your pocketknife and cut a huge snickerdoodle cookie in half: one half for you, one half for me. I wish that you were still here to teach me how to drive and how to play a proper game of tennis. Both of those things were your pride and joy. When I saw you in the hospital, I wanted to ask you if you felt okay but I did not have the words to do it. The last words you said to me were "I love you" and that will forever remain in my heart.

Love,
Alayna, age 10

Dear Cameron,

When you left to go to the hospital with your mother, I didn't know that it would be the last time I would ever see you alive. You were just thirteen months old and I never dreamed that your life would end so soon, especially after you had survived your time in the NICU after being born prematurely. We thought you were a fighter and that nothing could take you away from us, but we were wrong.

If only I had known, there was so much I would have said. I would have told you that I loved you, of course. I loved you so much. I don't think that you knew that, and I don't think I did either. I wasn't a good father in the short time that you were on earth, and that kills me. It was a difficult time for your mother and me, and I let it interfere with my thoughts and feelings. I can never forgive myself for that. More than anything, I wish I could go back and tell you how much I love you, but I can't.

I used to feed you your bottle and rock you to sleep every night before I would lay you in your crib. I loved doing it, but sometimes you would be fussy and wouldn't go to sleep. I remember one night I got frustrated and upset and it made you cry. I hugged you tight and said I was sorry, but I have always felt guilty for that time and the other times that I got annoyed with you for little stuff like that. I would give everything I have just to be able to hold you and rock you to sleep one more time, just for one night. I am sorry that I was so selfish that night.

If you had lived you would be eleven years old now. What a wonderful boy you would be, I'm sure. I wonder what you would look like, what you would say. We'll never know, but I know that we would be so proud of you and love you so much.

Oh, Cameron. Even now, your death hurts the same as it did the day you died. Nothing will ever make it better. There will always be a hole in our life where you should have been. When I think of all the ways that I failed you, it breaks my heart; it crushes me. Nothing will ever make up for your loss, nothing will ever soothe the pain that we feel when we think about you. Part of me still cannot believe that you were taken from us. Your loss was proof to me that life is not fair, that it is random, that all that you love can be lost in an instant. There is no God, there is no fairness, there is nothing.

Your brother, Christopher, I think, has been affected by your death, even though he may not quite remember it. One day you were there playing with him, the next day you were gone. I think there is a sadness about him because he lost you, even though he may not consciously know it. You have a sister and another brother now who were born after you died, who you never got to meet. I wish you could have met them.

Your mother has suffered terribly from your death. She blames herself for not saving you and there is a darkness in her soul that can never be cured. She loved you so much and seeing her pain makes me so sad. She will never be the same now that you are gone.

Little Cameroonie, my baby, my son. I miss rocking you to sleep every night while I fed you your bottle. I miss getting you out of your crib every morning after you woke up. I miss seeing you play with your toys and crawling around the house. I miss you so much, and I would give anything to tell you one last time how much I truly love you and how much I have missed you over the past eleven years. Please know that I would do anything to get you back, if only it were possible. Be at peace, wherever you are.

I love you,
Dad, age 44

Dear Brandon,

I miss you. I loved the time we played soldier. You are good at hiding. I had fun. You have a big heart. Thank you for watching the house and calling the police when that boy broke in. Remember how all of the soda was gone and all the ice cream was gone, too?

Love,
Sam, age 8

⁓

Dear Randy,

This past Saturday, we had a memorial service for you. You were only fifty-four and died suddenly of an aneurism. You left your wife, my daughter, and your two teenage kids and all the friends and family who loved you. It was so evident at the service that we all had wonderful memories and everyone had a "Randy story." I have thought in the last couple of days that we didn't tell you how much you meant to us. We assumed you knew. I hope you did.

I wish I had told you how much it meant to us that you became a father and trusted friend to our grandkids as they grew from gangly, shy preteens into such a fine young man and woman. So much of that was due to you and the love you gave. You were the perfect husband for our daughter, who had left a bad marriage and was unsure with no self-esteem. You helped return her to the confident, loving and capable person we had known her to be when she was younger.

You filled our lives with laughter, love and smiles. I hope we did the same for yours. I wish I had told you thank you more often for all that you did for us.

We have to remember to cherish those close to us and to tell them how much they mean to us. Give a hug or a pat on the back, tell a story, say I love you, write a letter to a faraway loved one, leave a note, and never, ever wait to say thank you for everything.

Love,
Lynn, age 58

Dear Na-Na,

I miss you. I know I barely knew you, but I hear about you and know how much you loved me.

I heard about how you cried when I was a baby because you were too weak to hold me after your stroke. I heard about you wanting my name to be Victoria because you wanted me to be your Little Vicky. I heard about you being one of the five people I would let hold me when I was little.

I might not remember much, but I do remember your warm house with the red brick fireplace and your big statue of the elephant that I used to ride. Don't worry, your big elephant is still with us as another memory of your life. I remember your bed with the big red fluffy blanket. Most of all, I remember being told you were dead. I remember not understanding why everyone was crying.

My mom and I were looking through boxes that you had given her. We found one box that had a whole bunch of smaller boxes inside each one. In the smallest box there was a note from you to Mom. The note wasn't long, but it was filled with love and old memories. Na-Na, that was so sweet of you. My mom really loved the note.

I'm really sad you left me before I got to know you. I can tell you were special because every time my dad talks about you he swells with love and joy. I miss you, Na-Na. We all do.

Love,

Vanessa, age 12

⌒

Dear Carly Marie,

I will never forget the first time we met five short years ago. You had on a lime green summer dress and I didn't know anyone could be that beautiful. I was so nervous to talk to you, but soon we talked every minute of every day and we went out every night that summer. I still have the notes you wrote me on paper towels.

I remember it like yesterday, when Emily told me you had a dress but no prom date. It took me four hours to finally get the courage to ask you. I didn't show it, but when you said yes, I exploded inside. When I was driving home that night, I yelled out my window, "I am going to prom with Carly!" I will never forget how gorgeous you were in your dress, and how I was breathless all night.

But seasons went by, and when we were in our senior year of high school, we went to different schools and we both became busy with college applications. We never found time to hang out anymore. You had a perfect 4.0 GPA and were accepted into the state college. You had everything going for you; your future was so bright not a star in the sky could outshine you. Simply amazing.

I will never forget the morning I woke up five long months ago. It was seven a.m. on the day of your graduation party, and I woke up to my parents calling my cell phone wondering where I was. I had stayed at my grandparents' house the night before because I got off work real late and didn't want to drive the extra ten minutes home. They sounded so worried and told me to watch the news. I turned it on and it said "Breaking News: 3 teens killed in tragic car crash." I fell to the floor. You, Mike and Jordan were three of the best friends I have ever had.

I miss you so much. It's not fair. My only regret is that I hadn't talked to you in months before the crash and that I should've been at the party you were at that night. Maybe I could've stopped you guys.

Your best friend,
Dylan, age 19

Dear Nanna,

It's been a little over a year since you passed away. It's Christmas tomorrow, your favorite holiday. You and Aunt Janice would always come over on Christmas Eve for dinner, and you would always give me the best presents. As I look back on it now, I remember the way your face used to light up when I opened my gifts; you had such a big heart, you had love for everyone. I'm truly grateful for the wonderful memories; you gave me such a magical childhood. I still think about you every day. I still feel as if you're going to walk through the door any second now: with your glasses on, your pink coat, and your brown velvet gloves.

Tonight when I took the dog out for a walk, I put them on. They are pretty old, but still warm and soft, and in perfect condition—just the way you kept all of your things. I smelled them to see if they still smelled like you. They did, but they smelled the way your house did after you got sick. It didn't smell bad, but it just smelled unhealthy in some way. Nothing compared to the warm and fragrant way it used to smell.

I loved your house, I always felt safe there. You always had time for me, for all your children, for anyone that needed anything. Sometimes I miss just sitting in the living room, just you, Mom, and I. I know that Mom misses you a lot, too. No matter how much time has passed, she'll always be your baby, and I know it still pains her that you're gone.

Lately, I've been going through a lot. I feel like I can't talk about some things to anyone. It's easy to feel alone and like no one cares, but I know I can always talk to you and you'll hear me, wherever you are. I miss you so much, but I'm so blessed for the beautiful time we shared together. I hope one day we will all be reunited. Until then, I love you always, and Merry Christmas.

Love,
Sarah, age 17

Dear Grandma,

I love you. I tell you this every day, but you don't remember. Every day, I tell you what school

I go to and where I live. When I come visit you,
I tell you what month it is, whether it is time to get
dressed, and how to get dressed. I make meals for
you and stop you from eating cottage cheese
seventeen times a day, because you don't
remember having had it yet. I give you baths and
brush your hair and tell you that yes, you have had
breakfast already. I love you so much.

I know you used to be so "with it." You used to
follow the stock market assiduously. You taught
yourself six languages, and learned English when
you came to America with your husband and little
baby, my mom. You tried to take good care of her,
even if you didn't always make the right decisions.
I know you were and are emotionally abusive to
her. I know that it is because of the abuse you
endured, the years of your life that you lost to
running, hiding, stealing bread, and trying not to
be killed that day. I know you love her, and you
just have no idea how to show it.

I love how you used to steal cookies from the
grocery store, and how you rip napkins in half so
as not to waste, and how your face lights up when
I come to visit you.

I just wish I wasn't losing you, bit by bit, every single day. But I want you to know that I will be there until the very end. I will bathe you and paint pictures for you and make you breakfast. I will tell you what school I go to every day, every hour, if that is what you need to hear.

I love you.

Your youngest grandchild, age 21

⁓

Dear Grandma Sharon,

I wish that when I talk to you face-to-face, I could tell you that I love you. I could tell you how kind you are and that you stand up for people, but I am too embarrassed to tell you. I could also say that you are a gift-giver and that even though you don't have enough money to give me, you give it to me anyways. I wish I could be generous like you. If you were sad, you could still make me smile. You've always brought the best out of people, including me. You have inspired me to do so many things. Now I want to inspire others.

Love,

Brendon, age 11

⁓

Dear Lou Lou,

I hope you are having a good life in Kitty Heaven. I wish that every day they serve you the best gourmet cat meals. Remember how, whenever I was sleeping, you would sneak into my room and bite my feet? It has been a year now and I would trade a million dollars to have you back. Your favorite food was chicken and that was also your nickname, "ChickenLou." If you ever came back, I would pamper you like the richest person in the world would pamper a pink Pomeranian. I know I don't believe in ghosts, but I wish you could come back every day whenever I wanted.

Your meow could echo a thousand miles. I wish I could hear you meow, again and again and again. You are still in the corner of the yard, lying peacefully and definitely not forgotten. If you could sneak into my room and bite my foot over and over, like a TV commercial you watch over again, that would be a miracle from all the heavens ever existing.

Bye bye, Lou Lou. I wish you the best.

All my love,

Julia, age 9

Papi,

I can't believe it's been six years. Six years of not hearing your voice. I still miss your jokes and your blow-up temper and then how you would get over it in five minutes. Dad, there are so many things I want to tell you, things I discovered after you died; so many things that I either didn't want to confront or was too selfish to deal with.

Dad, I'm so proud of you. I wanted you to know that. You came to the U.S. with absolutely no money at forty years old with a wife and child and restarted your life. Now that I'm a mother I can't imagine what it must have been like for you: no career, no money, no home. But you did it, Dad, and not only did you do it, you left Mom financially set, with a house paid in full and a retirement fund. I can't begin to tell you how proud I am of you. The fact that you did that working at a grocery store just blows my mind.

I was finally able to get a few pictures of your mom. Do you know that I had never seen her? I broke down when I saw them, because I realized

how important she was to you. I have those and a
few of you in Cuba as a teenager. Geez, Dad, you
never told me how handsome you were.

I'm really sorry I didn't take you out to dinner
more often. I never realized how much you
enjoyed it until Mom told me how much you
enjoyed eating out.

The boys are beautiful. Jonathan acts just
like you, it's almost scary. He's almost fifteen
and, as you can imagine, he and I get into some
pretty intense arguments. Then five minutes
later we're fine: like grandson, like daughter,
like grandfather. Mario is great; just a really good
kid. Alex got married and has a baby of his own.
Can you believe I'm a grandmother? You would be
so proud of them. That's what kills me. The fact
that you weren't able to see them grow up. But
I want you to know that they know what a
wonderful grandfather they had and how much
I love him.

I love you,
M, age 40

Dear Mom,

Your birthday will be soon, and I have been thinking about you a lot lately. I miss you and pray that you are happy and comfortable and maybe that God has given you a new body; one that doesn't hurt, that functions perfectly and takes you wherever you want to go. I hope that you have animals and little children around you, too. You would be ninety-two years old on the fourth of December if you were still with me. Amazing, isn't it? You haven't even been gone a year, but it does seem like a long time. So much has happened.

The renovations on your house are almost finished. I think you would like them, though I believe you would be very anxious at each new step. All the doors and two of the windows have been replaced. All the rooms painted as well, mostly shades of lavender and light pink. Even some curtains are up. Everything that is done makes me wonder what you would say about it. I know your anxiety level would be high, as is mine.

The months since your passing have been long and yet filled with concerns and worries. Still,

I miss you and Lily told me she misses you, too. I really don't think anyone understands. I think I am expected to just move on, and to some extent I am because I don't really have a choice. But at night, when it is quiet and I am alone, the sadness creeps in and even wakes me up when I am asleep.

You might like to know that I am writing a sort of biography about you and your family. I will try to complete it, mostly for my grandchildren and any nieces and nephews who might be interested. What I have learned so far is that I have come from a family of very strong women. Perhaps I have some of that strength in me. I sure hope so.

Larry and I have a Christmas log with live greens and a beautiful red Christmas bow to put on your gravesite tomorrow. I love you, Mom. Happy Birthday and Merry Christmas, too.

Your daughter, age 63

Dear Grandma,

You knew the key to my heart—good junk food and some talking. I loved how I'd always wake up to a breakfast full of bacon and waffles. You even let me drink all your Slim-Fast. Later, we'd make giant sack lunches and head to the park, or sometimes to the dock of the bay. We'd sit and eat our sandwiches, Cheetos and desserts, and talk for hours.

I wish we could still hang out like old times. I've grown up a lot. I graduated high school this past year and played a hell of a summer season. I'm taking a year off of baseball, though. It's hard but I have some things to sort out. I've had a few girlfriends and I wish you could have met one of them. She was beautiful with the sweetest smile in the world, just like yours was. You would have loved her.

It's hard to think about all the things I'm going to do in this world and know that you can't be there to share those times with me. You won't be there when I graduate college, you'll never be there for another home run or there to spoil me afterwards. You won't be crying in the front row at my wedding, or in the delivery room for my first child. You will never be able to see your grandson shape his life around the love that you taught him how to share with the world. But you will forever be in my heart and I will always feel at ease knowing you are watching me from above and guiding me through life.

Love you with all my heart,
G, age 19

⌒

Dear Lucy,

I've had a hard time forgiving myself for never writing this while you were in the hospital. You'd been there for months and I knew that the youth group and church had all sent you letters. I figured there would be time to sit down and think about what I wanted to say. The day I actually sat down to write you was when you passed away.

Lucy, thank you. Thank you for making church fun and interesting. Thank you for treating me as an equal regardless of my age. Thank you for treating me with respect. Thank you for honoring my confession about having an eating disorder and assisting me in getting help. I trusted you completely and still do. I know that, wherever you are, you know that there's a lot of love that's still being sent your way.

We still Facebook you—you can check. We sent you well wishes on the anniversary of your death and asked you what you thought of heaven. We sent you thank-yous and comments about missing you. I will always miss you, Lucy. As a friend and as a pastor. I haven't been to church since you died. It's just not the same. I still cry when I think about you, cancer, or any of the songs I listened to on the way to your memorial service.

I jumped in the lake today in a skirt and thought of you. Remember that time we convinced you that the water was warm and you jumped in, skirt and all? I brought that up at the service. Brian told us about the time you forgot Bryce at the rest stop and backed up down the breakdown lane to get him. Bryce reminded us of how you thought the Olive Garden restaurant was actually a field of olives and that they couldn't possibly grow up north.

But we all miss your laugh, Lucy. The halls of the church, of Horton Center, and our hearts are empty without it. I love you, Lucy. We all do. And I know I speak on behalf of everyone who knew you when I say it was too soon, too fast, and undeserved.

Shannon, age 17

HOW
FAR
WE'VE
COME

Dear Old Friends,

It has been a long time. I admit that is my fault. I cut off all of our communication because I was scared. I know you didn't know this, but I reinvented myself when I came to Oregon. I grew up getting bullied for being gay, and that made me cover up who I really was with you. I changed my look, the way I acted, and I became unrecognizable. I fooled you. I even fooled myself.

When we met each other, you were so welcoming. You really liked who you saw. Eventually, the jokes came about people like me. I laughed along, but deep inside you were hurting me, too. It was at that point where I started to not like who I was becoming, but I accepted it. I knew I wasn't going to be able to be my real self around you.

After high school, when we all began going our separate ways, I decided to go mine. I made up every excuse as to why I couldn't see you, and eventually, you all gave up. I am sure some of you wondered what had happened. I know some of you eventually found out that I was gay and reached your hand out to me. I shunned you again.

I was living who I really was and was afraid of the closed minds I had been hurt by before.

I am not afraid anymore. I love who I am and I am surrounded by friends and family who love who I am as well. It may be too late now, but if any of you ever reach your hand out again, I will put my hand out for you as well. I am sorry for not accepting it before.

Sincerely,
Ryan, age 28

Dear Lulu,

It has been twelve years since you left us and yet not a day or hour goes by that I do not think of you. Your absence is a hole in my soul that never seems to heal even the tiniest bit. If anything, the wound and void grow.

You see, so many wonderful things have happened since you left and I never get to share any of them with you. I know you watch from above, but that's just not good enough. Always, I want to call you first and share the good news. Or call you first for advice or just to listen to my rants.

But no, I cannot. Those opportunities have been taken from me as they have been taken from everyone whose lives you touched so briefly.

Ah, the moments, the phases, the gifts, the battles, the triumphs, and the new lives you have missed in our family.

Your nephew is so big now. So tall, you would not believe. Your niece that you've never met has been walking for a month now and I think that she is a gift directly from you and every day they both grow more beautiful.

Other family members have their ups and downs, but they are finding their paths, trudging along without you just as I do. Your favorite nephew became a teenage father a few months ago. I wonder what you would have said about that. Another is following in your footsteps and serving his country.

Your mother and mine. Well, Sis, this may hurt. She has not been the same since you left. She's no longer the mother we knew. Gone with you went her laugh, her wit, her strength, and her fight. With your absence they became grief, sadness, despair, and profound loss. I write this more for her than for myself. But do not take this on your conscience; her faith has served her well in her dark moments.

Lulu, this is supposed to be a letter saying things that were not said in time and I just wanted to take a quiet moment to catch you up on anything you might have missed from God's vantage point. Who knows, you may have had a hand in all the wonderful things and therefore know them already. But I really just wanted to tell you again how much I love you. How much I miss you. How you were just the most wonderful sister and beautiful person ever and I hope that you felt my love.

My love forever,
Prissy, age 34

Dear Mark Jr.,

I want to say I'm very sorry you are in foster care. I never wanted you to be away from me, never. I'm sorry your mother and I argued in front of you and your baby sister. I'm also sorry when you are sad and feel alone at times. I do miss you so much. Seeing you once a week is not any kind of time to spend with a son. I can't wait for you to come home and I promise to spend as much time as I can with you. You are my son and I want to be the best dad a bad dad can be.

Mark Sr., age 40

Dear Aaron,

You destroyed me. You took a strong young beautiful nineteen-year-old and ripped her out of me.

I thought you were perfect when we found out I was pregnant and you said you would be there, but how was I supposed to know that through it, you would be out cheating on me, drinking our money away? How was I supposed to know you would come home and fall and pass out right on top of me? I remember the night you fell on me so hard I thought you killed our unborn child. I remember the first punch. I remember being spit on and called a whore. I remember. I hate that you think you can say it didn't happen because you don't remember, that you must have been too drunk. That's not a man. You're not a man.

I remember being so scared of you all the time. I remember hiding in the closet during the day like a child. I remember feeling like a child. You took everything from me. You ripped it out and shredded it to tiny pieces that I can't find. Do you remember taking our son and locking him in the room with you? I remember showing up at your parents' to get help to call the cops because you wouldn't let us have a phone. I remember them telling me it was my fault. I remember being black and blue and bloody and it was still my fault.

You will never be able to take anything from me ever again. I have become happy. I have protectors in my life and I love them for their support. People love me, something you always said no one would do. You were wrong.

Leah, age 30

Dear Josh,

You were one of my best friends. I wish I could have been more patient and better to you. When you left, I felt like some of me was ripped out.

I only have the other part now. There are a few
new kids you would meet at church, and you'd be
more respectful of their unusual actions much
better than me.

I remember you smiled even when it was hard.
You figured out problems better than me, and
in a more calm way. You made me laugh with
the jokes you told. You were flexible about the
games we played and went with the flow with
cheerfulness. I remember when we played till
night and laughed to sleep.

I wish I could just at least have contact with you
in Chicago. I completely understand your dad's job
offer—I'm fine with that—but I hoped we would
chat on the Internet and we didn't. You were such
a great friend to me, though I didn't really return
the favor. Most of what I'm trying to say is, I am
sorry and I hope to see you more often.

Melvin, age 10

Dear Papa,

Growing up we were never too close. I was
always with Nina. She was the best grandma a
child could ask for, and the day she finally lost her

battle with cancer, my world changed. I had never realized what life would be without her. My birthday cards were now in your handwriting and only had your name on them.

Thanks to Nina, you did finally become a Catholic and just like she predicted, you were the best. Instead of living a life alone, you were at the church every day. You greeted people every mass, fed the homeless every month and even did the accounting. You taught me how to have faith and how to love. You never remarried after Nina, you never even dated. You were the greatest example of how a man should be.

You could fix just about everything. You and my dad put our wood floors in. You and my dad redid our kitchen. You built my desk and my first toy chest. You helped my family so much and you never gave up.

I just want you to know that you did a good job. Just like Nina said you would.

Love,

Kelly, age 18

Dear Mom,

For so many years, I tried to make our relationship a healthy one, but it never worked. In truth, I would never have stopped trying. When you finally cut me loose and told me you didn't want me in your life anymore, most of what I felt was relief. I don't have to try anymore. I don't have to pour energy into a toxic relationship and keep hoping for something better. I don't have to let you emotionally abuse and manipulate me anymore.

All I'm left with now is questions. Now I have a daughter, and when I look at her, I try to imagine her ever doing something that would make me stop loving her, and I can't. I loved her unconditionally, right from the start. Right away, I knew that I would do anything to love and protect her, the way a mother should. So why can't I remember you ever telling me you loved me? Why can't I remember you ever giving me a hug and not making some uncomfortable joke out of it? Why did you spend all of your time trying to tear me down, instead of building me up?

I'm not angry anymore, if you can believe that. I survived you, and I'm doing well. I just can't understand why it had to be so hard. Life is hard enough without having a hole in your heart where the love of your mother should be.

It turns out that when you released me, you did the best thing for me. So maybe in doing that, you for once acted out of love, whether you realized it or not.

Anne, age 36

~

Adam,

This will be a hard year for me. The anniversary falls on Easter Day. It's a day I take off work, drive down to sit at your gravesite, and then go back to bed. The one thing I do look forward to this year is going to your nephew's first birthday on the tenth. Oh, how you would have loved him.

Times may be easier now but you're always on my mind. I don't think that will ever change. Thank God.

Your dad,

Allen, age 51

Dad,

Happy Birthday! You have been away from us now for a little over ten years and I think of you often, probably more now than ever, as I have a beautiful young baby girl. I'm sure you would have loved her. Now that I am a father I realize so many things that I never did when I was young. Especially how hard it can be, and yet how lovely it is at the same time each and every day. I finally understand that the love of a child is by far the greatest love there is in the world, even though my daughter cannot express this to me. I see it in her eyes every time I walk through the front door. That brief moment is the best part of my day.

I look back now and realize that I was not the perfect son and did many things I regret, but what I do remember is that no matter what happened you always loved me. Perhaps the words weren't said often, but as a father, I understand that now because it is the actions of a parent that can speak volumes about their love. While heaven is far away, I know you are close by every time I pick her up and look into her eyes. Thank you for teaching me everything. Unfortunately, I may have never said it enough when you were alive and I wish I could now, but I am so proud to have been your son. I can only hope my daughter will feel the same about me. I miss you. Happy Birthday!

Your son,
Christopher, age 37

Dear Mrs. Musselman,

English has been my favorite subject since ninth grade. I had a wonderful teacher that year that I adored and still revere today. She taught me that Shakespeare's plays were risqué and still relevant. She praised my writing content. She instilled in me a real love for research.

Then I had you for tenth grade English and you made English class the most dreaded period of my day. Instead of praising my creative flourishes and the intellectual substance of my academic analysis of *The Sun Also Rises*, you harped on my grammar and punctuation errors. I would get papers back from you that were full of angry red marks.

Behind your back I mocked your "old-school" ways, including your out-of-date, mushroom-shaped haircut, tiny glasses, and Frankenstein shoes (which I now think might have been orthopedic). Yes, I realized, even at the time, that what I was doing by criticizing your superficial peculiarities was mean, but I was hurt and striking back. Of course, I had the ridiculous hubris of a fifteen-year-old girl who thought her writing was beyond reproach.

Even when you complimented me and told me I had a real talent for poetry analysis, I couldn't allow myself to appreciate you. I found all the mechanics that you seemed to value so much mind-numbing. I wrote flirty letters to Luke instead of taking notes while you diagrammed the parts of speech of sentences on the blackboard. Yet, the constant repetition of rhetorical rules must have seeped into my subconscious because my writing did indeed improve. Of course, you never did manage to convince me that the parenthetical asides I love so much were unnecessary and irritating, but I consider them more carefully now than I used to and I guess that's something.

After my junior year of high school, I went on a school-sponsored trip to Spain and you were one of the chaperons. You impressed me not only with your extensive knowledge of all things Hemingway, but also with your enthusiasm for Renaissance art and flamenco dancing. I started to like you, in spite of myself. You were still old-fashioned, but I could see how much you really cared about your students when you confided in me that I should watch one of the girls on the trip because you suspected she was bulimic and you were worried about her. (You were right, by the way.)

After I graduated, I started to appreciate the Socrates maxim "The only true wisdom is knowing that you know nothing." I also became aware that sometimes the things that bored me, or seemed trivial, were actually some of the most important things for me to assimilate. I'm pretty sure I saw you at my five-year reunion. I think I thanked you. I hope I did. However, at the time,

I still didn't fully appreciate the gifts you'd given me.

In started working as an SAT tutor in the 1990s as my "day job." When asked if I could work with students on the English and Writing portion, I found that grammar coaching came easily for me. I work with students teaching them syntax concepts. All those classes with you, Mrs. Musselman, have helped me to earn a living for the last fifteen years.

In 2002, I went back to grad school to get my MFA in creative writing. I thought of you quite frequently during that time and composed parts of this letter in my brain but never wrote it. Then, in 2006, I read in a Lancaster Country Day School alumni newsletter that you passed away. I felt the sick twinge of regret deep in my stomach. I wrote a letter to the school expressing my great esteem for you and my gratitude for all you taught me, but it was a vague eulogy, unworthy of you.

Please accept my apology for being an unappreciative student in tenth grade. I use the concepts you elucidated for me every day of my life. Thank you for persevering with us all and teaching me despite my resistance.

Sincerely,

Debby D., age 37

⁓

To my very shy girlfriend,

I just want you to know that I love our infrequent hugs where it is so hard that we stumble around the room holding each other, like an awkward waltz. There are times when you're not around and my arms ache for those hugs.

It's been many months and we haven't even kissed on the lips yet. I said I would wait until you felt it was right, and I've kept my promise. I want it to feel right, too.

Love,

Your extrovert, age 16

⁓

Dear Papa,

I never would have thought the time between us would be cut so short. I love you, and I miss you so much. The whole family could never picture life like this. Remember how you would always care about everyone's well-being, and if they were right with God or not? Giving all your time ministering and guiding everyone, you came across in the just direction and really showed your true colors.

As you already know, I'm sure, my daughter, your granddaughter, was born on April third of last year. She is so beautiful. She has your features—your wonderful smile, the pretty blue eyes and that same unique scent on your forehead. When I used to brush your hair, that scent stuck with you. I loved it.

Papa, as you can see I'm screwing up. Yeah, I'm in jail writing this letter, but it's all Jesus because it has actually brought out the best in me. It has given me the chance to sit and reflect. So far I have spent a decent month in here. It has been harsh, but I have been asking you and the Lord for strength and I appreciate it greatly.

I don't think I ever stressed the fact that you were my best friend and my greatest teacher, with help from above of course. You have done an outstanding job as a father and even more so as a friend. You will always shine through me in my journey to bring up my family well in these next few years. I will see you in my prayers. I love you and miss your warmth.

Your loving son,
Abraham, age 23

⁓

Dear Grandma,

When I was a little girl, you were my caretaker, another mommy for me to love and learn from. You and Grandpa took my mom, my sister, and me in with all the love of the heavens and helped Mom raise me and Layla together. I remember being little, and looking up at you smiling down at me. I barely remember living anywhere else before that, and I could never fathom, at that point in time, living any other way. Even when we moved in with my stepdad, I always liked to come visit, to sit in my old room or to watch *Jeopardy* with you guys.

You are my grandmother, the one who goes for walks, always so fit and healthy. You are amazing in every way.

I love you so much. I just want you to know that. Although it seems I don't care, as much as it seems I try to ignore your condition, I am very well aware—and I am scared.

I'm scared because I don't want to lose you.

I hate the cancer for making you so weak, and to think that you might not live to see me graduate makes me want to go knock on Death's door and have a small "conversation" with him. I want you to live as you should, as you always have—healthy, able, loving. I want you to be there when I go off to college, when I get married, have children. I want you to be out there, laughing and clapping. I want to see you in the crowd when I'm acting, watching me with that smile on your face.

It feels so wrong, to see you sitting there looking so tired. You've never looked tired before.

I love you, and I want you to live as long as is comfortable. After that, I will spend every day living to the fullest, like you would want me to. I will live every day like it's my last, and when my last is up, you had better be waiting by those pearly gates to give me a big, healthy, grandma hug.

I love you,

Grace, age 18

Nicholas,

I remember our inside jokes and the times we'd burst out laughing at nothing at all. I remember falling asleep together on my couch and waking up in each other's arms. I remember the trips we went on. You knew I was terrified of flying, so you held me as the plane lifted us off to Mississippi where we'd do our charity work together. Whether it was shoving food into each other's face or crying on each other's shoulder, I knew I'd found a best friend in you. There was nothing you wouldn't do for me, and there was nothing I could hide from you.

The first time you hit me, I had no idea what to do. We were walking down a hallway together and I must have said something wrong, because next thing I knew, I was on the ground. My Diet Coke seeped into the carpet and my bag spilled clutter next to it. You stopped for a second before you kept walking. I knew you had kicked me down, but it had to have been an accident, or at least you had to have had reasoning behind it. I was wrong.

When I found someone else, you were angry. Your verbal attacks intensified, and each hit led me closer and closer to the ground again. I was scared of you, so I went back to you again. Fortunately, the verbal attacks lessened. But the sexual and physical violence did not.

You hate me now. You won't say a word to me. And when you do, I see you flinch. You told everyone that your liver was destroyed by the alcoholism that I instilled in you. I assumed you said it because you thought it made you look cool, to walk around saying someone destroyed your life, as if that was an excuse for why you are the way you are. It's not an excuse, Nicholas. I have to live with the real secrets, and I'm the one that has to keep quiet about them. I'm the one that has the scars, the bruises, and the e-mails. It's nothing to be proud of, and it's certainly not something to show off. The truth is, it hurts. It hurts a lot.

If it makes any difference, I am so sorry for anything bad that I ever did to you. You are a beautiful human being underneath all of that hatred and confusion. And although I only caught a glimpse of the beautiful human being you could be—the one that loved those children as much as I do, the one that stood up for me when no one else did, the one that always knew how to make me smile—I am still so grateful. I do not believe that you have it in you anymore, but I am so glad that I am the one that saw that side of you, even if it was just for a fleeting second.

But it is my time to move on now, Nicholas. And I will miss you. I will miss you so much. I can never forget the times we had together, both the good and the bad. I will always be here to support you, even if that means being invisible watching in the distance. You are loved. Never forget that, never doubt that. I forgive you, and you are loved.

Haley, age 17

⁓

Dear Grandpa Otto,

I want to thank you for reacting as awkwardly as you did to my first period. You would never believe what a wonderful turn my life has taken because of it. I know you remember the moment that we locked bug eyes (me on my water skis and you in the back of the boat) when we noticed the stain on my bikini bottom. I'm sure you remember our silent drive to the pharmacy. You stayed in the car because you were too embarrassed to guide me to the right aisle. Later, while I was peeing, you cracked open the door, dangling the cordless phone as if it were infected. "You should call a woman," you whispered. I stayed in the bathroom for an hour while you paced outside. I was too ashamed to come out. I imagined you shaking your head, confused and wondering what in the world a widowed old man could offer to a hormonal teenager like me. The rest of the week water-skiing with you was hell.

What you don't know, and what I wish I could tell you, was the surprising effect of your silence. It made me want to ensure that no other girl would feel as alone as I did. It made me ask the other women in our family for their first period stories. I don't think I had ever seen the older women in our family giggle before (Aunt Nina has gold teeth!). I learned that my best friend got her period on the day of her bat mitzvah. I got into Gloria Steinem and Eve Ensler;

I read *Ms.* magazine. While my friends played video games and illegally downloaded music (I did some of that, too), I collected period stories. For five years! This February, they all got published into a book. My high school classmates will remember me as that period chick, writers will ask me questions about publishing, potential employers and dates will Google me and stumble upon a video of me gesticulating how to insert a tampon. I will go on the radio and answer mothers' concerns about how much of a celebration is too much, respond to teenage girls' questions on why they are sleepy when they get their period, and attempt to help fathers struggling with how to broach the subject with their daughters. You've changed my life in the weirdest and most wonderful way and you'll never know, Otto. I feel like I've done something already to define myself and make the world a tiny bit better (or at least a little less awkward). I know that you would be blushing right now, wherever you are, if you knew how often and how proudly I tell our story.

Love and miss you,
Rachel, age 19

Dear Mom,

I'm pretty sure you died peacefully. It didn't seem like you were in any sort of pain. I had to tell you that it was okay for you to go. That was very painful for me. After you died, I went downstairs to the hospital chapel. I hated God and everything about Him.

Your funeral was beautiful, Momma. Daddy preached it and I sang "How Great Thou Art," your favorite hymn. You wouldn't have wanted so many people to make such a big fuss, but I think it was worth it. Actually, you probably wouldn't have even been able to make it to the funeral. You would have been at our house getting things ready for the dinner and directing all of the other women that wanted to help you.

It's only been seven months, but I've gone through so much since you went home. This summer I went a little crazy—well, a lot crazy. I drank and smoked and did so many bad things. I got a tattoo. I know I promised to make you proud. I'm so sorry for those things, Momma. I really am.

Senior year started in August. Since then, I've been very good. I think I've made my peace with God. I'm living for Him now.

I got the lead in the fall musical. We performed *Rags to Riches*. It was the first time ever that that show was put onstage. It was incredible.

I have a boyfriend now, Mommy. His name is Jake and he treats me so well. We've set limits to what we're going to do and what we won't. I'm doing things right this time. I don't want to mess up with him. He's amazing for me. We've only been together for about a month now, but I think the plan is to stick together for a while. He tells me I'm beautiful all the time. You'd think he's pretty cute, too.

Problem is, he's Mormon. So, I'm not getting my hopes up for anything. I guess my philosophy is, God brought him to me for some reason, and I just have to wait to learn whatever lesson that is.

I miss you every day, Mommy. I don't think it will ever get easier, and to be honest, I don't want it to get easier. I feel like if it gets easier, it's like I'm forgetting you. I'll never, ever forget you. I wish

you were here for all of these things that I'm going
through. I wish you were here to see me graduate
and go to college and get married. All of those
things will be bittersweet for me now. But I know
that even though you aren't here in body, you're
always watching over me. You promised you'd
always be here, and I believe you.

I love you, Mom.

Love,

Molly, age 17

THANKS,
FOR
EVERYTHING

Dear Jan,

Do you remember me? You were my high school guidance counselor about thirty years ago. I was the too-skinny girl who kept coming back to your office long after I was first called in to see you for some wrongdoing I cannot recall.

Thank you from the bottom of my heart for caring enough to guide me in what was one of the worst times of my life. I think of you sometimes, especially when people ask me how I survived my troubled teenage years. I think, "I don't know if she knows how she made a difference in my life." I don't know if you knew what was happening in my home life or if you were intuitive, but your kindness and empathy made me feel cared for and worthy.

As I recall, you helped me apply for the job at the university bookstore my senior year, helped me get into the vocational technical school that same year, and helped me apply for Youth Conservation Corps when I was fifteen years old. When classmates tried to beat me up after school, or when they teased me for being poor, I'd come into your office and talk to you about my problems. You didn't ask me what I did wrong or tell me to fight back. Instead, you listened and gave me advice on how to handle the bullies. You treated me like I was a regular person. I sure didn't feel regular. When I didn't feel picked on, I felt invisible. I needed adult help to let me see there was life after high school. I needed your kindness, your empathy, and your guidance to make it through.

I'll never forget this: seeing you writing on some form you had to fill out for me—maybe on my admissions form for Youth Conservation Corps, I don't quite remember—that I was an above average student. That was the first time my intelligence was acknowledged. My parents never even looked at my report cards, didn't ever help me with homework, and I certainly didn't have good grades. Now, in my interactions with others, and especially with children, I model that same behavior: I let them know I think they are above average, even if they may not see themselves as such. Doing so will give them something to strive for, as it did me. I worked hard my senior year, after dropping out of school altogether my junior year and having to make up credits. I graduated from high school, whereas neither my twin nor my younger sister did. Maybe it's because I had you to help me succeed.

I live in Eugene, Oregon, now. I have a daughter who is going into high school in September. She was bullied a lot in elementary school—the subtle "If you don't do this I won't be your friend" kind of bullying that girls specialize in—and I worry about her in high school. Girls get bullied a lot more than people realize. But she has a mother who is prepared and knows what signs to look for and who is available, unlike my mother was.

I suppose you were like a mother to me, now that I think about it. Please know that you made a difference in someone's life—a huge difference. I am now a healthy and successful woman, who is happy in life. And I don't let anyone bully me!

Karol, age 34

Dear Mom,

I have always wanted to say thank you for making me breakfast. And for adopting me. I do not know where I would be if you hadn't. I am

.appy when you help me when I need it. I am
thankful that I am here with you. I love you, Mom.

Love,

Emily, age 9

∾

To my husband's birth mother,

I wanted to write this letter to you to let you
know that nearly forty-three years ago, you gave
birth to a baby boy who has grown up to be a
wonderful man. He and I have been together for
ten years. Over those years, I have asked him about
you. Part of me really wishes he would search for
you. I don't want you to think he is not interested—
I think he is curious. But for whatever reason, he
has not been compelled to search for you, and
ultimately searching for you has to be his decision
and not mine.

When I ask him what he would like to tell you,
he always says that he would like you to know
what a wonderful life he has had and that he
doesn't have any anger or resentment against you.
He really has had a wonderful life. He was adopted
by a very loving couple who gave him every

opportunity and cared for his emotional and physical needs. His dad passed away a few years ago, but his adoptive mom is still alive and well. She has always encouraged my husband to feel comfortable to look for you if he wanted to. I know she is so grateful to you for what must have been such a difficult decision.

My husband has a marvelous sense of humor. He's also a big animal lover and has a soft spot for strays. His biggest talent is his musical ability. He plays multiple instruments and has written several songs for me. He's also very smart and a voracious reader. Above all, he is a decent person who has all kinds of friends and gets along with all kinds of people. One thing I've always respected about him is how he really gets to know people for who they are. He isn't swayed by money or titles.

As I write this, I am seven months pregnant with our first child—a boy. Being pregnant has made me think about you more than I have in the past. I feel so connected to our baby boy even though he hasn't been born yet, and I can't imagine how difficult it must have been for you all those years ago to give your baby up, not knowing what was going to happen to him. I feel connected to you through this baby. Your blood is running through him, and that's a powerful thing.

I hope someday my husband will decide to search for you, and I hope you want to be found and get to know us. If I never get a chance to meet you, I want to use this letter to tell you thank you so much. Thank you for being brave enough to give your child a good home. Thank you for giving him a chance in this life. Because you did, I got to meet him. Because I met him, I got to marry him. Because I married him, I get to have his child. I'm so happy I got to marry him. I just adore him. I think you would, too.

Thankfully,
Jennifer, age 33

⌣

Dear Mrs. Gabriel,

I'll never forget the beautiful toy railroad set that your son, Horst, got to play with each Christmas. Your husband would only put it out in December, and each time he did, I was invited

help. I learned from you that life is precious at should be treated every day as if you could only live for that one more day.

With the last days you lived, you wrote some wise, life-experienced, heart-wrenching stories in your diary. I read those today. By the time I finished the stories you wrote, I saw how wonderful you truly were and how much I have missed.

Your husband also has something like the lovely story-telling qualities I found in your diary entries. Whenever he comes to our family gatherings, he finds someone new to tell the story about the time he killed a rattler, or about the time he discovered a field full of flying ladybugs, making the grass look blood red, or about the time he shot Mrs. Puddles's window with a shotgun and didn't get in trouble. He also talks about the time he finally realized that without you, his life would never be complete again.

I sometimes stop and wonder how we would have gotten along. I really would have loved to have met you, to sit outside your house and feed the birds like I heard you used to do. But what I

I would enjoy the most about you was your
ıse of adventure and love of nature, which are
.he parts of you that I see in me.

Even though I never knew you or met you,
sometimes I wonder why I know so much about
you. I know my mom tells me many stories about
your life, but I also feel part of you in me every
day. Every time I swoosh a basketball shot, or
flawlessly play a concerto on my violin, or even
when I am reading a fiction novel, I think about
how you only lived for forty-five years. This is
why I no longer dread going to school or taking
tests. I try to enjoy life more than I ever thought
possible. No matter where I live, what I do, or who
I meet, I will always live in wonder, joy, and
adventure, trying to be exactly like you. You lived
your life to the fullest, complete with love and
happiness. Now, I can only wish my life will be
half as joyous as yours was.

Your granddaughter, age 16

⌒

Ryan,

I don't even know where to begin. You were
always my best friend. I never had an older

brother, but you were always exactly like a
brother. I still think of you that way all these years
later. How long has it been? Fifteen years? Every
time I hear Alanis or Jann Arden, I think of you.
I wonder how you are doing. Did you marry?
Do you have kids?

Though I am gay, you never, ever made me feel
self-conscious about it. You never even brought it
up. Being like family, it was never an issue and I
always had great respect for you about that. If I
ever needed a boost in any way, you were there.
No questions. I hope I did the same for you. You
will never, ever know what you did for me. I
honestly don't think I would have made it through
without you. You know I would drop everything
and help you if you needed it.

Even if we never see each other again, you are,
and always will be, the best big brother I never
had.

Eric, age 39

⌒

Dear Grandpa,

It has been six years now since your death.
I wish I could have spent more than twelve years

of my life with you, but it truly does feel like I did. I have so many memories of you. I always say how the first memory I have of my life was when we were still living next to you and Grandma and you guys had been over for dinner, and as you were leaving you looked at me and winked. I remember trying to wink back, at the mere age of three, and failing horribly. Such a simple memory, but it's my most treasured one because it involves you.

I found a letter from you a couple months back. You had written it to me for my tenth birthday. It said how you and Grandma would start depositing money into my college savings account at each of my birthdays from then on. At the end it said, "Can't wait, front row at your graduation in 2014. Love you forever and always, Grandpa." I have never in my life cried as much as I did after reading that sentence. It is because of you and Grandma that I am attending the university of my dreams and getting an incredible education and college experience. I am sorry that you will not be at my graduation in 2014, but I promise to make you proud throughout the next four years so that when you look down on me from above as I receive my diploma, you'll be smiling.

Love you forever and always,

Your freshman-in-college granddaughter, age 18

⁓

Dear Mom and Dad,

I know our relationship has always been difficult. I can't pretend to have ever been an easy kid or even always respectful. I'm argumentative, defensive, dramatic, impatient. But the biggest thing that I am is underappreciative. Sure, you guys are my parents. It's natural you'd do a lot for me, right? Any parent would go to any length for their kid, right? Well, sadly, that's not always the case. Your own stories remind me of that. Thankfully, Kim and I lucked out. You guys would do anything you could just to help us out.

It really sucked being sick. Constant trips to the family doctor to get throat medicine. Countless visits to the emergency room, only to be told to go home. Finally getting admitted, but still no clear sign of hope at the end of the tunnel. It sucked for me being sick, but I can't imagine what it did to

ys. I can recall how terrible I felt and
ed. I can't imagine how you guys felt seeing
our little girl practically withering away and
doctors unable to help.

I honestly owe my life to you guys. Especially
you, Mom. I was mad at you at the time, but if you
hadn't told that nurse that my chest was hurting,
who knows if they would have figured out
anything. The temporary pain was worth it, and
I admire you for knowing you were doing the
right thing, despite the glares I shot at you. And of
course, you too, Daddy. With all of your newly
acquired EMT knowledge, you could give them
much more detailed and helpful symptoms than
I ever could. That made a huge impact on treatment.
Thank you both.

But that was just the start. You guys visited me
every single day I was there. Eight straight days of
hospital visits; sometimes even multiple times a
day. You stayed as long as they would let you, and
waited while I had tests and procedures done. You
guys brought me food and my little comforts from
home such as Corner and my books. You made

sure I was taken care of by washing me off, bringing me comfortable clothes, and washing Corner when I got sick on it. It's all these little things that I don't think I really thanked you guys for. You guys called out of work and canceled appointments to be by my side while I slowly got better, encouraging me through the depressing realization that I wasn't going to Australia.

And, as if all that wasn't enough, Daddy, you were there almost all day for three days in a row, waiting for the moment that the doctors released me back into your care. Mom, you had to give me injections for two and a half weeks. I wish I had a picture of your expression when the woman said she wasn't coming every day. But, despite feeling sick yourself, you did it.

I know I never will say how much I love and appreciate you guys as much as I should. But I am really gonna try. Hell, if it wasn't for the love and dedication you guys showed me, I might not even be here today.

I love you both so very much,

Alyssa, age 20

Dear Coach Ben,

Thank you so much for coaching me. Without your help, I don't think I could have made it this far in my swimming career. Thank you so much.

Without you, it feels like there is a giant hole in the team where your place was. Everybody really misses you, especially me. I can't explain how much we all hope that you come back. Even though you pushed us really hard each day, I think you are an amazing coach and an even better friend. Each day, all I can think of is when you're going to come back, or *if* you're going to come back.

I hope that you know that I am extremely grateful for your help and I want you to know that you mean so much to me and the other Thunderbolts. I really, really hope you come back soon.

Sincerely,
Arden, age 10

Dear Music,

Thank you for giving me a sense of peace. Thank you for a way out, an escape nothing else would have given me. Thank you for being there, for getting it.

Thank you for giving me an outlet to expel everything I can't keep inside. Thank you for having endless possibilities, letting me know that nothing was crazy to think or wish.

I owe you for my sanity, my happiness, my hope.

Sincerely,

Me, age 16

~

Dear Shadee,

I thank you for everything you have done for me. You play a lot with me, and you showed me how to do something when I didn't get it. When I was being bullied, you came and stood up for me. I didn't know how to thank you. I hope we'll have fun for the rest of our lives.

Love,

Parsa, age 10

~

Dear first grade teacher,

You helped me persevere through hard times. When I opened a book, my heart would start racing and I would be excited, but then I remembered I couldn't read. I tried but I couldn't. Every time I opened a book, it got worse.

You suggested that I go to an eye doctor and that solved the problem. Now I can read, all because of you. Because you didn't give up on me. I never got to say thank you before you left.

Kayla, age 11

~

Dear Disney World,

Thank you for everything. Thank you for providing me with a haven of hope and imagination and dreams where I didn't feel death or pain or tears (except tears of joy). Thank you for not letting me fall. Thank you for bringing perfection to life.

Thank you for treating me like a kid and for not letting me forget what I was when I was a child. Thank you for letting me grow up at my own pace.

Sincerely,

Kelsey, age 16

~

Mitzi,

You were our housekeeper and my nanny for the first six years of my life.

You were the most important person in my young years. I saw more of you than either of my parents.

Each weekday morning, you walked me to kindergarten and then picked me up again for lunch. We walked towards our apartment at the edge of the Danube Canal through the colorful streets of Vienna. You prepared my lunch, tucked me in for a nap, and later played games with me till you prepared supper. I took your presence and care for granted.

After Kristallnacht, you disappeared from my life and I missed you terribly. I cried and prayed for your return but soon we were forced to leave our apartment and I was sure you would never find us again. One cold February afternoon, there was a knock on our door—a knock always sent shivers of fear into our souls—but when my mother opened the door, it was you, Mitzi. You had a spray of lilies of the valley in your hand and a Happy Birthday greeting on your lips for me. It was my seventh birthday and I was filled with joy for the first time in many months. Two months went by when, once more, there was a knock on the door. We were not as fearful that day in April, since we had the precious papers that would allow us to emigrate to the U.S.A. in a few days. The narrow, dank room was filled with a shipping box for our belongings to be sent ahead.

You came into the room and announced that you were taking me for a trip to the "Prater," the huge amusement park in the middle of Vienna. It was against the law for Jews to enter the park but you put a knit hat on my head to hide my dark hair and we were off for the adventure of my young life. You took me on the rides, including the huge Ferris wheel, treated me to ice cream (a rarity in those days), and we watched the marionette show in the plaza. I didn't get a chance to tell you how much I admired your courage and appreciated your love. Having contact with Jews was forbidden, and taking a Jewish child into a public place could have resulted in the arrest of everyone in your family as well as dire punishment for yourself.

I would very much like to thank you for giving me the only really good memory of my

childhood days in Vienna and restoring my faith
in humanity.

Ruth, age 76

⌒

Dear writers who share their personal letters,

I want to thank you for what you've given to me
and to the world. I've read touching and
heartbreaking stories of could-haves and should-
haves. I've cried my eyes out from the sadness of
the unpreventable tragedies you write about. I
want to tell you how much you are empathized
with, and how much I respect the humanness of
your writing. I need to thank you.

I personally am too young and too lucky to have
any great regrets. There are some. There are things
I'm ashamed to have done, which I will have to
deal with. However, I haven't had the opportunity
to do (or leave undone) many regrettable things
yet. For me, most of those decisions are yet to
come. And I want to thank you for helping me
understand how to make better choices when the
time comes.

I need to show my grandmother, Mummu, that
I love her. The amount of love she has for our

family is difficult to grasp. She's not one to express her emotions in words or hugs, but she's always there for us. She needs to be shown how much it's appreciated. And that lonely girl from our class. I should talk to her more often. I will talk to her more often. I'll help my friends understand their worth. I'm going to develop, examine, and reexamine my ideas and values, and act upon them. I'm going to stop making excuses and start living properly.

The Internet is full of inspirational quotations and pictures. How many times have I seen those words, *carpe diem*? And is this the first time I've realized the importance of the meaning of those words, of seizing the day? No, but I have a tendency to forget. You, dear letter-writer, reminded me. You reminded me of some of the most important things in life.

Thank you.

Sincerely,

A reader, age 17

Acknowledgments

I can honestly say that this book would not exist without all of the incredible people that supported me and the project.

First and foremost, I have to thank my family. Mom, thank you for hanging flyers on bulletin boards between business meetings and telling anyone who would listen about each and every step I took on the journey. Even more, thank you for rubbing the stupid out of me and for being my *Rocky* theme song whenever I needed you. Dad, I wouldn't have gotten anywhere without your legal advice and for always reminding me that "It's not the size of the dog in the fight, it's the size of the fight in the dog." If I ever get contacted about a catchy song for the project, your "Watchu Woulda Said" rap will be the first one I mention. Jason, thank you for always being there. You've had to endure endless conversations about letters, site analytics, and editing, and I have desperately appreciated your ability to pretend each one was just as important as the last.

Sisters, thank you for posting articles about the project on your office walls, accompanying me to interviews, and asking your teacher friends if I could present in their classrooms. I am thankful that I have two sisters—and an adorable niece—who care so much about me and what I'm doing. Grandpa, I am honored that you have allowed me to share your story and I am grateful for the encouragement you've given me. Grandma would be proud of us. Uncle Peter, thank you for accepting me into the family club of authors; your support helped me believe that it was possible. I would also like to thank my wonderful friends who were always there to listen, motivating me to keep moving forward and to challenge myself. I couldn't have done this without you.

David, I approached you early on when the project was still very young. You believed in the idea and what it could become, coaching me through its progress and teaching me along the way. You gave me the best introduction to the publishing world that I could have ever imagined, and I would not be here today without your guidance and encouragement.

Thank you to Brittney at Hudson Street Press for knowing what I wanted to say before I could think of it myself. You had the remarkable ability to revive details of the project that I had somehow forgotten, and I'm so thankful that you helped me remember and soak in those special moments. I am lucky to have you as my editor and cannot wait for what's to come.

I also want to thank every organization leader that allowed me to present my idea. Specifically, thank you to Joe Pishioneri for being the first person to respond to my inquiry letter, telling me that I had "fire in the belly" and that if I maintained my fire, I would get many things done in life. Thank you to Kara Wendel, Anna at VOA, and Michelle Lockhart at Findley for the multiple rounds of group participation. Thank you to the journalists and radio and TV producers who helped spread the word so that I could hear from people I never would've reached otherwise.

Lastly, to all of the fearless writers: thank you for taking a chance on me. Without you, this would be nothing. I will remember each and every one of you, always.